Wanderings of a Captive Mind

John E. Beerbower

Published by FastPencil Publishing

Wanderings of a Captive Mind

Fourth Edition

Copyright © John E. Beerbower 2019

All rights reserved. No part of this publication may be reproduced, stored in a retrieval system, or transmitted, in any form, or by any means, electronic, mechanical, photocopying, recording, or otherwise, without the prior consent of the author.

Sale of this book without a front cover may be unauthorized. If the book is coverless, it may have been reported to the publisher as "unsold or destroyed" and neither the author nor the publisher may have received payment for it.

http://www.fastpencil.com

Printed in the United States of America

Table of Contents

Preamble vii
A Journey? 9
An Open Letter to John G. 21
"First Things" and Abortion 25
Science and Public Policy 35
A Look at Climate Change and Public Policy 40
    Some Background 41
    Climate Science 45
    The Big Questions 58
    Conclusions? 68
A Proposal for Tax Reform 75
    Setting the Stage 75
    Revisions to the current US System 77
    A Note Reflecting the Current Politic Climate 83
    Concluding Comments 86
"AntiReligion" and Sam Harris 87
On Nationalism 95
Good Citizens and Moral Leadership 101
    "Good Citizens" 101
    Political and Civic Leadership 103
    The Decline of Moral Authority 106
    The Decline of Virtue 108
    The Decline of Heroes 111
    The Role of Community 112
    The Future? 113
A Note on "Systemic Racism" 115
    "Systemic Racism"? 117

>A Brief History of Slavery 120
>Racist Law Enforcement? 125
>Income, Homeownership and Wealth 130
>Some Other Facts 139
>Government Policies 147
>And, So... ? 152

Advice to my Children 155

Preamble

Breathing,
Easy.
Easy to take for granted.
Does not require consciousness.
The primitive brain can do it,
As long as the neurons transmit
And the muscles respond.
So easy,
Breathing.

I experienced an early warning in Cambridge during the summer before my diagnosis (2014). I jumped into the deep end of the pool, into rather cool water. I surfaced and began treading water. To my shock, I found I could not breathe, not at all. Nothing. I paddled to the shallow end, where I could stand. Air. It was frightening, and inexplicable.

Now, I understand. The diaphragm would not respond, and my chest muscles were otherwise occupied keeping me afloat. Over the next seven months, I unknowingly experienced the consequences of an unresponsive diaphragm. REM sleep was impossible; if I fell into deep sleep, I stopped breathing. Thereafter, I slept with a BIPAP ventilator. During the day, I could breathe on my own.

I moved to Alexandria in 2015. And, the muscles steadily weakened. Soon, I needed breaks with the ventilator on. The breaks got longer. And longer. After a stay in the hospital, I came home pretty much tied to the machine, except to eat and drink.

I have only experienced that inability to inhale again when I have had a mucus plug in my lungs. We have now learned to use the cough assist to deal with the blockages at home; but for about a year, our recourse was 911. The paramedics could not do much except hook up oxygen, but the ambulance ride up a very bumpy Duke Street always did the trick. Unfortunately, I could never convince them to turn around and take me back home! So, hours waiting in the ER always followed.

These days, I primarily just suffer from a shortness of breath without the ventilator, an inability to take a full breath and a growing feeling of suffocation. I am pretty comfortable at an oxygen saturation level in the high 80s, then it gets challenging. And, yes, the lights do get brighter.

My neurologist told me that the end was very likely to be respiratory failure. She said it is very peaceful!

I suspect she was assuming sufficient morphine.

A Journey?

May 2018
3 years, 2 months

In March 2015, I was diagnosed with ALS/Motor Neuron Disease; although, I had already been experiencing what I know now to be symptoms for at least two years. The diagnosis had a rather muted impact on me at the time, because of the state I was in. In the prior weeks, I had lost my sense of taste and smell, was rapidly losing weight, found my speech somewhat slurred, would suddenly drop off for a moment in the middle of speaking or while driving (which I stopped doing) and was experiencing hallucinations.

As it turned out, the problem was prolonged deprivation of REM sleep. The pulmonologist explained that in the prior months, my diaphragm had weakened so that when I fell into REM sleep, I stopped breathing and immediately woke up, that is, went back to normal sleep. So, even though some days I would sleep comfortably for 12 to 14 hours, I was totally deprived of the deep sleep my body needed. As a result, my bodily functions were shutting down.

At the very beginning of May, I experimented with a ventilator (a BiPAP) while sleeping. After seven hours, my symptoms almost totally disappeared. I rapidly became myself again, and the enormity of the change in my life that was beginning struck me pretty hard. In discussions with my daughter, I concluded that, for my life expectancy of 2 to 5 years, two years was unacceptably inadequate while five years seemed tolerable.

The reality, however, is that this disease is very individual and not very predictable. In fact, ALS is a rather unique chronic disease. There is typically no significant pain, there is no cure or meaningful treatment (there are some things that can statistically slow the deterioration, but there will be no noticeable impact), the deterioration of the muscles is relentless, the order in which the muscles are affected is not predictable in advance and the rate of progression will be relatively constant for any particular individual but will vary greatly from individual to individual. Falls are a real danger while one continues to try to walk. The wheelchair relieves a lot of anxiety. In part, the variations in the progression of the disease from one person to the next is a result of the lack of available treatments with common side effects; so one experiences the effects of the disease only, and not of any common side-effects of standard treatments. This all means that the victim is sentenced to a period of waiting and watching as strength and functionality disappear, with crystal clear awareness yet minimal (serious) discomfort.

One relative advantage of ALS compared to other fatal illnesses is that the victim is generally guaranteed some opportunity to make plans, communicate with family and friends and get one's affairs in order. That opportunity to me was very useful and relatively comforting. At the same time, one is confronted with making plans for a future of indefinite duration.

I have found that the key to a sustainable life with ALS is to find the right balance between living for the moment and planning for the future. For me, it has been essential to force myself not to think further ahead than is necessary in order to be able to make timely arrangements for things that are to be needed. That means that, compared to my prior life, I have become much more focused on the here and now. My goal became to find a way to get joy and meaning from each day.

That was essential for several reasons:

- First, serious contemplation of the likely course of future events is intolerable and, therefore, needs to be avoided.
- Second, if you can bear today, you may feel with some confidence that you will be able to bear tomorrow—taking each day at a time (the progression is gradual and very incremental, so that the changes from one day to the next are not noticeable).
- Third, things that one may feel today will be unbearably terrible in the future may likely turn out to be manageable after one has suffered through the intermediate downward steps.
- And last, if you cannot find a way to enjoy today, then there is no point in worrying about how many more tomorrows you may have.

It is really a strategy for survival.

Before talking more about living for today, let me explain what planning is necessary. There are things that will be necessary at some time, so it is prudent to make the needed arrangements in advance. Adequately in advance, but not excessively so. Walkers, portable wheelchairs, ramps, toilet aids and the like can be ordered online for delivery within 3 to 5 days. An adjustable bed can be obtained in one to two weeks. An electric chairlift for stairs can be obtained and installed in 2 to 3 weeks. However, a power wheelchair, customized, can take up to four months from order to delivery. Renovating a bathroom to make it accessible may take three to four months. Other equipment for which you want insurance coverage require planning since it takes time for approvals.

My situation was a bit more complicated than usual. I was living in England when I was diagnosed. My daughter and I flew to New York to meet with my son and daughter-in-law to agree on a plan. We booked an extravagant trip for the four of us. We decided that I would buy a house in Old Town (Alexandria, Virginia). My daughter and I shopped online from England and selected four possibilities, which my children then visited in early June. I negotiated the purchase, closed at the beginning of August, directed renovations and interior decorations and arrived to move in at the beginning of October, with the furniture all in place. In the meantime, I sold my flat in London. My daughter packed up and shipped our belongings from England.

Thereafter, my activities were a bit more typical. I sorted files, organized memorabilia, revised my will, tried to make my financial affairs understandable to my children. I then began the process of making the necessary arrangements and obtaining the necessary equipment to enable me to live at home for the foreseeable future. By late 2016, I was using the power wheelchair regularly, but I could still ride up the stairs on the lift. Two years later, I had to move to the ground floor full time. So much for planning.

The more important process was that of learning to live in a new and different way. I tried some guided meditation but quickly progressed to my own, independent form. I found I was able to spend significant periods of time with my mind disengaged, floating from thought to thought, letting each go in turn. Often, I did so with my eyes closed, but equally often I would sit and watch the birds, the movement of the leaves, smell the plants and earth, follow the blooming of the flowers and observe the other activity in my garden. I am fortunate enough to have a lovely garden and beautiful rooms in a historic house. So, there are multiple places where I can experience the outdoors, enjoy my paintings and otherwise appreciate pleasant surroundings.

I now talk less and listen more. A useful development in and of itself, and probably something I should have tried long ago.

I also became much more emotional. That is, my emotions became much more a part of my daily life, an important part. And, I have become much, much more empathetic. I am truly saddened by adverse things that happen to other people. And, I feel a much greater connection to humankind than before; the old me tended to define my identity in contrast to others, not as part of the common experience. (While I am accepting of my fate, I find it quite unfair that others are similarly afflicted.)

I find that I seem to be completely reconciled to my current situation. It is a sharp contrast with me at 13 bemoaning how unfair it was that I needed glasses! I do not know what happened exactly. In part, whining is an indulgence, a luxury. Greater hardship makes it seem pretty pathetic. Unlike the younger me, I do not ask: "why me." Indeed, the more pertinent and penetrating question seems to be: "why not me." I reject the claim that it is "unfair." It just "is." Maybe, I am finally starting to understand the Book of Job.

I have been reading almost a book a week, watching operas through "Met on Demand" and struggling to continue to do some writing. However, much of the time, I just sit and let my mind float, while my body experiences the sensory perceptions of sight, sound, smell and touch. Often, I can feel the breeze, sometimes cold and sometimes warm. This serene and passive interaction with the world was a substantial change for me from my prior life. While I used to think constantly about the future and plan meticulously, I now largely avoid thinking of anything more than two to three days away. Somewhat surprising, I find this to be a pleasant and almost satisfying way to live.

Almost satisfying.

But, there are two interrelated issues that challenge me. First, there is the enormous amount of work required to get me up and keep me going. I am actually quite embarrassed by the resources involved in my daily maintenance. Of course, I, unlike 99% of people in America, can afford it. Second, there is the question of what purpose is really being served by keeping me functioning in this manner. How do I justify to myself the commitment of so many people's time and energy to enable me to continue to sit and enjoy. What am I able to contribute? What is the purpose, *e.g.*, of continuing to learn when I will not be able effectively to communicate my thoughts to others?

Of course, I am aware that I am providing employment to several people and helping them support themselves and their families. But, somehow, that seems like a rather meager source of meaning for my continued living. And, the enormous burdens that my daughter has assumed haunt me. I cope with that by refusing to allow myself to focus on the long-term implications.

At the same time, I have come to recognize that I am still able to engage in acts of kindness, to listen, to empathize, to encourage, to support and, perhaps, even to inspire some people around me in their own daily struggles. Moreover, I have gotten to know my children much better, partially filling a significant gap in my prior life. I have also spent more time with my siblings in the last 3 years than I had in the prior 50. That contact has put me back in touch with my early years—my "roots". And, I have met my granddaughter (Hannah, born in March 2016). I have participated in her christening, been able to see her grow, been able to hold her.

So, am I still relevant? I am still a participant in life. That is something. Is it enough? At the moment, yes; but longer term, I don't know. For now, my goal is not to focus on things more than a few days out. Each day, one at a time.

September 2018
3 years, 6 months

It has all become more complicated. The "fly in the ointment" is that I am apparently dying more slowly than I had expected. I vividly remember steeling myself for what I expected was my last dentist appointment (for a cleaning). A couple of months later, the same for a haircut. Since then, I have been back to the dentist twice and have had 5 more haircuts.

My daughter is largely responsible. She has done an amazing job of investigating, analyzing and understanding what is going on. Even the doctors take advice and instruction from her. She has kept me going, physically (as well as emotionally). But, that success has a "cost". A coping strategy that was good for a period of months is not necessarily satisfactory when looking potentially at a period of years. Also, the continuing burden on my daughter looms as a much larger cloud. I realize that for three years

I occupied myself with preparing to die. Now I must find a way to continue to live and to do so with a rather bleak and potentially short future ahead of me.

I feel again that I need in my life some goals or objectives to provide the prospect of a sense of achievement or progress. Yet, my ability to do things continually diminishes. And, I am physically less comfortable much of the time than previously, when I could usually rest in a pleasant state at any time. Finally, of course, there are the periodic moments of crisis with the accompanying struggle, stress and fear.

However, I am quite happy that I made the effort to persist in getting *Limits of Science* published. Over the past few weeks, reviewing what I have written, I have been rather astonished, as I have discussed a bit with my daughter, by how much of me is reflected in the book: my personality, my tone, my attitudes, many of my beliefs, my methods of thinking and analysis and probably more. I do not think I was aware of that aspect of the drafts while I was writing, and I certainly did not remember it while I was going through the publishing process.

In any event, I feel good to be leaving such a significant part of myself behind.

January 2019
3 years, 9 months

I now have a grandson (Jeffrey, born in December)! I have been able to hold him. And, I have also been able to continue to watch my granddaughter learn to walk and, then, to talk. Also, she has now started school. In fact, Hannah talks nonstop. She also rides with me in the wheelchair.

May 2019
4 years, 2 months

Occasionally, I think that I caused this illness. Too often, I had often said to myself, "Oh God, I am so glad I do not have a chronic illness. I could never stand it." Perhaps, His patience wore thin; I can almost hear Him say, "Sure you can. Just watch."

However, some mornings, many mornings, when a new discomfort or problem arises, I say to myself: "You must be kidding. Enough."

Nevertheless,,

> "...I've come this far
> And I ain't givin' up.
> ...I've dreams blow up
> in a cloud of smoke.
> ...but I know somehow
> Some day the sun
> will find some way
> to shine down on my face.
>
> I pray for a stronger back.
> I pray for a bigger heart.
> I pray for the will
> to keep on walkin'
> When the way is dark... .
>
> I don't pray for a lighter load.
> I pray for a stronger back."
>
> Don Williams
> "Stronger Back"

I pray for things that prayer can deliver.

September 2019
4 years, 6 months

Another dentist visit and 3 more haircuts.

Also, several more trips to the hospital. Each time I am hospitalized, I return worse off. I bounce back, but not to where I had been. I suppose it is partly the inevitable trauma from whatever caused the hospitalization. But, the lack of sleep, poor food and general stress involved with a hospital stay all contribute. The nursing schedules are arranged so that you never get more than an hour of uninterrupted sleep. For years now, I have also needed my own caregiver in the hospital, because I can not press the call button; and, even if I could, I can not answer over the intercom.

Yet, if anything, I feel healthier now. But, I need more and more help; I can now do virtually nothing on my own, by myself or for myself. I cannot even safely be by myself. As a result, I have no privacy at all. It is tiring, but I have become much, much more patient (most of the time).

However, I am still able to "drive" my wheelchair and get outside. Over the summer, I have regularly gone to the Saturday morning farmers' market. I love the smells and the colors. I enjoy the hustle and bustle and the people of all ages. There are often many children (who stare and, sometimes, wave). I have also gone to church several Sundays. I very much enjoy the music, I bask in the sense of community and I feel inspired by the worship. Fortunately, I have a good friend to accompany me. And, I expect to be able to help celebrate my daughter's 30th birthday or, as she prefers to say, her second 29th birthday!

My daughter writes:

> *"Coming out of a period of back to back illnesses—*
> *another infection staved off by my gamble—*
> *made out of exhaustion more than anything—*
> *to treat empirically before he got sick;*
> *there we all are at home in the kitchen.*
> *He's off the BiPAP, drumming his fingers*
> *on his lap table, eyes closed,*
> *taking in Don Williams*
> *the way Don could only ever hoped.*
> *We look at each other—everyone pauses.*
> *All of us there, day in, day out; night in, night out,*
> *sharing a grin that only we understand.*
> *This is why we are here,*
> *it is the only thing that matters.*
> *This is why the world turns.*
> *This is what makes the pain bearable."*

March 2020
5 years

Curiously, I have been managing better for several months—I should say "we have." No hospital or ER visits. Issues have been dealt with effectively at home. Unfortunately, the current pandemic has put a strain on the "team" here. Yet, the people around me are doing exceptionally well. My routine has not changed that much. Social distancing was my normal! But, the current crisis paradoxically has strengthened the sense of community around me. Of course, we are painfully aware that I am in the highest risk category. Is it just a matter of time?

So, I find comfort in Billy Budd's aria sung while waiting to be hanged, toward the end of the opera of that name:

> "Oh, I'm contented. ...
> Don't matter now.
> ... I am strong.
> And I know it,
> And I'll stay strong.
> And that's all.
> And that's enough... ."

Benjamin Britten, "Farewell to ye, old 'Rights O' Man'!", Act II

I have been mainly watching and listening now for months. One passing thought: I think that I have always disliked most hypocrites; second most, cheats (not "honest" thieves, but deceitful, manipulative gamers of the system). Maybe, I most dislike cheating hypocrites. Most cheats are hypocrites, but not necessarily vice versa. I have been wondering what having these feelings reveals. I cannot work it out.

A second, I have now come to believe that the greatest virtues are empathy and humility—reflected in the recognition that "there but for the grace of God, go I." (Empathy is what I think is meant by Christian love for "thy neighbor.") It has probably taken me too long to come to this awareness. It may come naturally to some people; but, for me, suffering was necessary to the process of realization.

I feel better for this insight.

August 2021
6 years, 5 months

Wow. It has been over a year, actually some 15 months. And, a very strange year, at that. I stayed in my house and garden or my daughter's property for about 10 months. After I was vaccinated, I got to get around a bit, saw all of the new construction—residential renovations, new condominiums. Unbelievable how prosperous Alexandria has become. New cars every where, most with either no tailpipe or at least two. It is probably well that most of the country can't see the affluence the Federal government delivers to its own!

I have not been hospitalized for over a year now, the longest stretch since 2016. That has changed things a bit. I rather miss being surrounded by the big EMTs and firefighters. I usually got one ambulance and one firetruck, but sometimes two fire trucks. The rest I do not miss. This progress is a result of improvements in my care and trying to do everything at home. The absence of hospital visits, however, has changed my outlook. I used to go from crisis to crisis, happy just to survive each. Now, I feel a bit lost without such challenges to overcome. The days just roll along.

I wrote that I had become more patient since this disease, but I suffered a setback as I was losing the ability to communicate by speech. The frustration was astounding. I was accustom to assisting in my care with suggestions and sounding alarms. Then, increasingly I could not make myself understood, at least not without great strain. But, I am learning to cope. Now, I try just to watch what happens and wait for the consequences. They are generally not so bad?, certainly better than the frustration and chaos of me attempting to help.

I have been focused this past year on pain in my muscles, noticeable only when touched or pressed, like during stretching or massage. Many of the spots are deep in a muscle, like soreness from overexercise, but other spots are right at the bone and quite painful. The sharpest pains are in several areas right at the surface, just beneath the skin. Presumably, they are symptoms of muscle deterioration. I have watched for patterns of progression without success. Sometimes, my eyes tear-up, not from the pain but from the fact of the pain, from what is happening to my body.

I used to love to lie in a tent with the flaps down, feeling the breeze, listening to the sounds, without worrying about mosquitoes or flies. If I had an itch, I could leisurely decide whether to scratch it knowing it was not likely to be a bug (although, maybe a spider). I am referring, of course, to modern tents, not to those heavy, smelly canvas tents we used to use. I can no longer enjoy a tent, but a screened in porch is almost as good, especially the one at the Bay. I can not scratch an itch, either. I just will them away, which is pretty effective with an ordinary itch, but not so useful with a bug.

One bright spot has been watching the growth and development of my grandchildren. They accepted quite easily my situation—the wheelchair first, then the ventilator and mask. Of course, the mask seemed less strange when everyone started wearing them. I do not know what their parents have told them, if anything. I mainly observe, of course, while they play in the garden. Frequently, they say "Grandpa, follow me" or "Come see what we found." And I do.

What has amazed me is their mental and verbal development. It is fast, so fast and relentless. I failed to appreciate this astonishing human capacity in my own children, probably because I was so busy trying to interact and not really watching. Humans are truly astonishing: perceiving patterns and relationships, inferring causality, deriving conclusions. And, this capacity is clearly discernible by age 2, if the child is talking. For example, I recently used the suction machine in front of them, which I had avoided. Jeffrey proclaimed "just like the dentist," where he had been for the first time the week before. I am very happy to have been allowed to observe this phenomenon first hand.

A lot has changed over the past five years, and I think I have adjusted. What I miss most now are drinking coffee together with Yami in the mornings, especially at the Bay on the deck outside of my bedroom, and sipping wine together with my daughter, also especially at the Bay. Companionship and some conversation. Now, it is: someone takes the mask off, turns the machine off, I take a sip from the cup or glass someone holds for me, the person turns on the machine, puts the mask on, I breathe. Repeat.

Still, better than wine through the feeding tube!

Two milestones today. First, I have passed 700 miles on my wheelchair. I had been averaging 250 miles a year, until the pandemic. It has taken 15 months to go the last 100. And, second, l have just finished typing this entry, all done using only my eyes. Thanks to TobiiDynavox, my newest bit of equipment.

So, what will tomorrow bring?

Advice for fellow travelers

- The greatest contributor to survival and comfort is capable and attentive caregivers. But, unless one has incredibly generous family and friends, that is very, very expensive. At a minimum, one needs an effective, persistent advocate. Probably because of Medicare procedures, everything requires at least one level of outside intermediary. It is exhausting and potentially misleading. Hospitals depend on routine:

One size fits all. It will not fit you. One must be constantly watching; you will be unable to do it yourself.
- Try to avoid getting cold. The muscles stop working. I was advised several years ago not to take hot showers because they sap one's energy. I find that, to the contrary, they help my breathing and general mood. But, cold is really debilitating.
- Stretching the muscles and motion help. Pressure is also satisfying. Regular massage is not so useful, but vibration from shaking or percussion (thumping) works very well to provide some relief without sharp pain.
- Exercise? Well, while you still have muscles that are unaffected, exercise can encourage those muscles to take over for some of the affected muscles, prolonging the ability to do things. However, I did not perceive that exercise actually helped the deteriorating muscles.
- If you are going to use a ventilator with a face mask, get as many different mask styles as possible and try to get used to each. They all put pressure on your head and face, but they each affect different spots. So, you will want to alternate masks regularly. You will have soft, tender spots all over, like an apple that has bounced down some stairs, but you should be able to avoid pressure wounds, which are very difficult to treat.
- While you can still talk, establish routines and signals that will facilitate your care when you can no longer speak. You can even create some useful instructions on a device you can activate by touch or by eye. Then, pray that your caregivers do not change!

Blessings!

An Open Letter to John G.

To John G. and our Classmates

June 2015

I recently returned from our 45th reunion last month, and I expect not to make the 50th. So, the time seems right to undertake a task I set for myself in the summer of 1967–a belated pseudo-apology, really more of an apologia.

First, some background. I grew up in a small town in Michigan and finished high school in southern Ohio. I was not the first of my family to go to university; both my mother and my father had graduated from Ohio State. We were economically comfortable and conservative. Because of my parents, I was able to attend college with no scholarships and leave with no student debt.

Nonetheless, Amherst College was an overwhelming experience for me. It was the students–their levels of academic preparation, their accomplishments, their life experiences, their self-confidence. I retreated into my protective shell and set appropriately modest goals for myself for the first year: middle of the class academically, some friends, maybe join a fraternity. My principle preoccupation, however, was with the lack of girls.

I lived in Pratt; unfortunately, I now think, in a single room. The room was nice, but my neighbors in suites were all immediately members of pre-formed groups. I was increasingly desirous of feeling like I fit in with the Pratt group, being recognized by them. Dorm-identity was strong; although, I could not understand it then (or now, for that matter): A dorm assignment that said nothing about who I was or who I had been was at best an arbitrary basis for group loyalty.

I also developed a huge admiration for and envy of a couple of the dorm proctors. They had everything. They had status at the College, the attention and respect of my classmates, nice rooms and girls.

Then came the night that I have often thought of with deep regret.

A dorm proctor of whom I was in awe, but who was from the north stairwell, knocked on my door in the south stairwell and said that they needed my help. I should have felt suspicious; instead, I was overjoyed. I pulled on a T shirt and, as we ran down the hallway, was told that we are going to shave John G's beard. I know many people will not be able to understand that I had no reaction to that information—not even the most obvious three questions who is John G, why shave his beard and why me? As to the last question, the answer is obvious: I was big. And, easily manipulated.

I had participated in two "beard shavings" already before Amherst. So I was experienced (actually, both had been chest shavings). These events reflected the exercise of collective action as an expression of camaraderie that would solidify the group's self-identity and deter deviant behavior. It was a declaration that the targeted member was being a "dick" and that that was the responsibility of the group. It was a means of engaging in discipline with the minimum of humiliation, positioning and moralizing. So, the facts that I did not know who he was or what he had "done" seemed of minor relevance. (There were rules. No blades. No biting. No fun or amusement. Everyone participating. And, quick dispersal when the message had been delivered, meaning rarely were any beards or chests hairs actually shaved off, just chopped up a bit.) A rather primitive ritual, I know; but ancient parts of our brain are still very much with us.

However, this event was importantly different. First, as I should have immediately recognized, I was not a part of the relevant group. Second, as I soon after did recognize, John G. was not either. These two facts made the event different, and particularly ugly.

Arriving at John G's room, I realized that another large fellow (from the central stairwell) and I were the designated "enforcers", while the people who presumably had a "beef" with John G formed the audience. The event was short-lived. Some hair was cut off, and the victim fought desperately. After a few minutes, the other guy and I returned to our own stairwells.

It was over, except for the disciplinary proceedings.

To my surprise, several students who were in the audience for the event offered explanations, effectively taking responsibility as the leaders. Neither I nor, to my recollection, the other guy was even asked why we participated.

In the subsequent weeks, there was the expected fallout—expressions of outrage, accusations of anti-Semitism, demand for punishment and expressions of support for the victim. Oddly, no one ever indicated that they were aware that I had been a participant. (Two years later, John, somewhat tongue-in-cheek, complimented me on my own, rather new beard, suggesting to me that he knew and remembered.) I do not then, and still do not, know the motivations of the organizers of the event. I do not think I had yet even met John G, and I barely knew the members of the "audience", who also lived in the north stairwell--a whole different world. Certainly, I was not motivated by any animosity toward or prejudices against John.

Over time, I think that what most bothered me, apart from my own weakness, were the actions of the dorm proctor as a ring-leader. Although, I recognized that I had been "used", I consciously felt no resentment about that fact. I had made the decision to participate, and I was ashamed of the decision. I have never fantasized that I could have stood up and prevented the event. Maybe the me 30 years later; but for the me at 18, that was beyond the even conceivable.

(As an aside, I was not generally attracted to pranks or group antics. For example, during the infamous October water fight, I remained in my single room with the lights out so as not to invite attacks from the outside. I viewed the activities that occurred as being unreasonably dangerous and destructive. I did not then regret my lack of participation, and I am still left unmoved by the fulsome anniversary reminiscences of the class.)

Curiously, at a recent reunion, I had breakfast with the other guy who provided the "muscle". I raised the subject of the event, for the first time in 48 years; he claimed to have no recollection of it, to not know what I was talking about.

This note, I know, would be a very belated but also quite inadequate apology to John. I write it, really, as an exercise in attempting to understand an experience that had a lasting impact on me. This was not the last conduct of mine that I have regretted, but it was the least ambiguous. Subsequent troubling events were more complicated, and the virtuous alternative actions less clear.

I assume that the event had a lasting impact on John G, as well. I can only hope that the consequences were not entirely negative, despite the pain that he must have suffered at the time.

"First Things" and Abortion

I did not take a class with Hadley Arkes while I was at Amherst College; although, I knew him pretty well since he was effectively a *de facto* member of the Economics Department (presumably, because it was the one bastion of conservative to moderate thinking at the time).

At some point, I did read at least part of his book *First Things: An Inquiry into the First Principles of Morals and Justice* (1986). *First Things* is a work of moral philosophy, in which Prof. Arkes sets out and defends his positions. I cited it as a source for a handful of propositions of philosophy in my own book three decades later, *Limits of Science? Important Things We Do Not Know About Nearly Everything* (2016), I used Prof. Arkes and his book as a source. I did so largely as a matter of convenience. There were other options for the same points.

Background

Shortly after writing my book (just before publication), I became aware of substantial on-going criticism of Prof. Arkes among members of my class at Amherst, which was celebrating its 45th reunion. The vitriolic comments were directed mainly at his positions in opposition to homosexuality, gay marriage and abortion. So, I rethought my choice of authorities.

In criticizing Prof. Arkes, these classmates pointed to statements in which he supposedly equated homosexuality with other forms of behavior that were uniformly perceived as immoral or uncivilized. (These statements were not in his book but in more recent writings of articles and commentaries.)

I assumed that Prof. Arkes was using an established form of logical argument to attack the proposition at issue (*reductio ad absurdum*). The argument is that if the proposition at issue can be reduced to a proposition broadly perceived to be absurd without crossing any principled lines of distinction, then the propositional issue must be incorrect (or, in this context, immoral). (More typically, the argument is presented in the form that a proposition is true when its negation leads to an absurdity.)

While, in some sense, since the advocate is saying that he sees no principled distinction between the propositional issue and the absurd or immoral proposition, he may be said to be arguing that they are equivalent; but, I think he is really posing to the reader the question of identifying the principled distinction—where to draw the line. To me, that is an important difference. The invited response is not the condemnation of the author, but the answer to the question. However, his essays were admittedly quite blunt or worse.

In any event, all of this led me to go back and reread *First Things*. I wanted to see what I thought of the arguments he made therein. Not so much, it turns out. But, then again, I had also criticized his arguments in my *Limits of Science*.

First Things

The opening argument

In his book, Prof. Arkes builds his argument for "necessary truths" on the following construct: He asks, is the proposition "there is no truth" a statement that is true or false? If it is false, then there must be some things that are true. If, instead, that statement is true, we then will know that there is at least one statement that is "true" and, given that, there may well be more. Thus, Arkes says, it must be the case that there are some "truths".

How satisfying is that logical exercise? To me, not very. To say that it is "true" that "there is no truth" does not obviously lead to the conclusion that there is "truth". Indeed, if there is "truth", then the proposition must be false. More importantly, however, if it is the case that "there is no truth", then it is not meaningful to demand that one declare whether that proposition is true or false. The reason is that if there is no truth, then the distinction between true and false is meaningless. If "truth" does not exist, then the adjective "true" is simply inapplicable.

Prof. Arkes also argues that it is a matter of "necessity"" that "two contradictory propositions cannot both be true". He treats that proposition as a matter of *a priori* truth, that is, something we know to be true independent of our life experiences, "knowledge" with which we are born. This "law of contradiction" plays a significant role in his subsequent arguments. He repeatedly attempts to show that each of various positions inevitably lead to a contradiction, which he claims disproves each of those positions.

I have a problem here as well. I have trouble seeing how the "law of contradiction" can exist or have meaning independent of or before language. The reason is that the propositions must be set forth, and they can only be set forth in language. I can imagine that *homo*, pre-language, could have understood that two inconsistent states could not exist simultaneously. For example, something cannot be both alive and dead, or it cannot be both day and night. However, contradictory propositions must be set forth in language.

So, can something simultaneously both "exist" and "not exist"? Can something both "be" and "not be"? Can something be both "true" and "false"?

Presumably, Prof. Arkes says definitely not. Well, apart from the fact that modern particle physics and quantum mechanics can be interpreted as providing affirmative answers to all three questions, these questions can only have meaning in "context". The answers will depend upon what the "something" is, on the perspective of the observer or multiple observers (possibly with different perspectives) and upon the meaning of the words in quotation marks (exist, be, true) and their supposed opposites. This is not so mysterious; it is the stuff of which many riddles are made.

THE APPLICATION

Next, Arkes asserts that the fundamental moral principles are "necessary truths" because of the related propositions that man is capable of reasoning (the basic elements of logic) and man has a moral sense, that is, a recognition of the difference between right and wrong. In other words, man uniquely among known living species is able to reason about moral propositions and to understand the concept of "justification". That characteristic, he asserts, entitles human beings to special treatment. For example, based upon the assumption that all people are "created equal", it is morally wrong to deprive a human being of life or liberty or, presumably, property without "justification"–without a logical explanation founded on a concept of justice or of right and wrong.

Prof. Arkes also seems to suggest that one can establish the existence of a necessary truth based upon an argument that failure to see that principle as a truth puts one on a slippery slope that will lead to clearly unacceptable results. The proposition would be that if conduct A is acceptable, then there may be no logical basis of distinction to assert that conduct C or D is not acceptable. But, this proposition simply states the question of whether there is a basis of distinction; it does not answer it.

I agree that man is (apparently) uniquely capable of reasoning about matters of morality. But, I can only say that that is true once man has the concept of morality or right and wrong. Is that initial concept a "necessary truth"? My dispute is not with the notion of *a priori* knowledge (or even so much with the "law of contradiction"). I accept that we are born with the concept of causation, with a sense of the meaning of space and spatial relationships and with the notion of time. But, of relevance here is the question whether man is born with a moral sense, the concept of right and wrong, good and evil? As to that question, I find myself quite uncertain. Does the concept of the moral arise from our genetic make-up or from our cultural and societal experiences? Interestingly, one can "explain" the emergence of many of these *a priori* understandings or constructs on evolutionary bases, as characteristics capable of giving an advantage in survival and reproduction. Can the same be said for morality?

I can imagine some convoluted explanations about how a sense of "right and wrong" provided an evolutionary advantage for *Homo sapiens*, but it does not seem very compelling. A better approach to an explanation seems to lie in the area of community and societal organization. As man began to live in groups, it would make sense that a set of rules concerning behavior would give a group advantage in the struggle with other groups over limited resources. In fact, law and morals could even have played an important role in the family group; although, I would think that the given power hierarchy in the family could be sufficient. In any event, the suggestion here is that the source of morality may not be in the capacity of man to reason, but in the strong incentives for man to live in communities, in being a social animal. If so, would that take morals outside of "necessary truths" and place it in the category of a construct of society? Alternatively, its appearance as part of community life could be genetic, facilitating successful reproduction not directly but as a result of the success of the group.

It may be that child psychologists can answer the question of whether the moral sense is innate or culturally derived (and, perhaps, they have already done so). But, if this issue depends upon a factual investigation, then it is "contingent" and not "necessary". As such, matters of fact seem to be fundamentally different from what we have discussed as *a priori* knowledge. On the other hand, we identify moral reasoning as a distinguishing and unique characteristic of mankind. Presumably, were we to discover some other life form that also engaged in moral reasoning, the moral principles that apply to humans should be extended to that other life form.

Actually, I have recently read a book by a leading social psychologist, Jonathan Haidt, that addresses some of these issues. The book is *The Righteous Mind: Why Good People Are Divided by Politics and Religion* (2013). Based on the results of a host of empirical studies, Haidt asserts that the sense of morality appears to be an innate human characteristic, but the details of what is right and wrong are derived from the culture in which the individual is raised. Thus, *e.g.*, the scope of morality is much narrower in Western, individualistic societies than it is in Eastern, family and community-centered societies. As he says: "We're born to be righteous, but we have to learn what, exactly, people like us should be righteous about" (p. 31).

In addition, Haidt explains that these studies demonstrate that typical moral reactions to events arise instinctively. Thereafter, the person may engage in logical reasoning about that reaction, but the reasoning is most often an effort to articulate a *post hoc* justification for the moral judgement already made, not an effort to reach a judgement. This is not "moral reasoning" as Arkes use the concept.

I have already noted that the existence of an innate sense of morality could have an evolutionary basis arising out of man's social being. Similarly, specific moral rules could have "evolved" in the competition among alternative cultures. Obviously, however, these supposedly empirically-based conclusions are at odds with the philosophical views of Arkes (and Kant).

I do not actually know where to go with this line of thinking. But, it does seem to me that a credible case can be made that what Arkes calls "the first principles of morals and of justice" arise as a matter of logic from what we as a society have decided to identify as distinguishing characteristics of humanness. But, if that is the basis of the principles, then the principles presumably could change as the societal consensus changes. This approach is in direct conflict with Arkes.

THE CONCLUSION

Moving forward, Prof. Arkes observes that if these moral principles are necessary truths, then it is insufficient to say that "I will live by these principles but leave to every other person the decision as to what to do." The reason is that if they are truths, then logic demands that everyone be expected to abide by them (recognizing that there will be individuals who decide to break the rules). Obviously, society has many rules. But, that fact certainly does not establish that those rules are based on necessary truths, just as the fact that a principle is not reflected in a law of society does not mean that it is not a necessary truth.

As an aside, I would note that Arkes' conclusion about the need to impose moral rules on others is not a necessary implication of religion. For example, I do not understand Christianity to advocate that its views of right and wrong be imposed on others by law. Its religious teachings, as I understand them, are directed to the individual and to the individual's personal salvation; they are not to be forced on people but to be chosen by them. Christ's well known injunction "Render unto Caesar..." reflects the distinction between the world of government and law and that of the spirit and morality. The advice "Feed the hungry, clothe the naked" was not addressed to the State or the governing powers, but to individuals who were urged to give of themselves (not to redistribute the property of others).

Prof. Arkes' conclusions seem more in the nature of "natural law". As I understand it, "natural law" is based on the assumption that actual laws do or should reflect that which is morally right. But, what is the basis of that assumption? I did not find "natural law" jurisprudence very persuasive when I took the course 45 years ago with Lon Fuller. I still do not.

THE ISSUE OF ABORTION

Prof. Arkes devotes his final two chapters to the matter of abortion. I have considerable sympathy with his concern about the subject. It is difficult to articulate why the "taking" of the life of a newborn infant moments after birth (even through the failure to feed or provide shelter) can lead to charges of murder or manslaughter, yet doing so through affirmative action only weeks earlier may be perfectly legal. Nonetheless, I again have issues with his arguments.

He frames the question in terms of when the new life can be said to become "human", identifying various characteristics of the unborn fetus and looks at how those characteristics, when existing in a living person, are treated in the law. He notes that the law provides protection to persons with severe disabilities, retardation, mental illness, on life support and with other conditions that limit or prevent the display of characteristics that we would generally identify as part of being a full human.

Then, he says, why should the unborn sharing some of these characteristics be subject to having his or her life taken "without justification"?

By looking to the accepted legal standards, Prof. Arkes seems to assume that what is and has always (or often) been protected by the law are rights that are "necessary" as a matter of moral principle. Yet, that assumption seems to be resting on somewhat flimsy grounds. We know that the law sets forth many rules that have no or little moral content. In addition, legal rules are often shaped by pragmatic considerations, such as the benefits of having a "bright line". Finally, some of these legal rules have changed and continue to change overtime. For example, we have seen already, and it seems likely that we shall see further, some significant changes in the laws concerning suicide and assisted suicide.

So, if the question is when does an unborn child become a "person" or become "human", I do not find Prof. Arkes references to the legal treatment of various categories of individuals who have been born as very useful. In fairness, he does also discuss the difficulties of basing the test on various biological or developmental characteristics or stages. Scientific progress has pushed the conclusions of many of those tests earlier and earlier in the pregnancy. Of course, the embryo is "human" biologically from the beginning. I just do not think that this is the right question.

THE RIGHT TO CHOOSE

Most proponents of abortion frame the issue in terms of the right of the woman to make decisions about her own body. The law generally provides considerable latitude with respect to what one legally can do to one's own body, such as cosmetic surgery, decorative mutilations, and the like. In addition, although the law generally prohibits suicide, people are normally permitted to engage in extraordinarily reckless and dangerous activities where the likelihood of death or the risk of serious injury to health is significant. This argument is sometimes augmented by the assertion that in relation to the mother the unborn fetus it is really a parasite. Presumably, the suggestion is that a person has the right to eliminate a parasite. whenever the person so chooses. The "viability" standard implicitly reflects this categorization.

THE LAW IN OTHER AREAS

With respect to the question of the obligations of the woman to the unborn child, I note that the law generally provides very few duties or obligations of one person to come to the assistance of another. For example, one has no legal duty to feed a starving person (and, it is generally illegal to steal food in order to save one's life or the lives of one's children), to assist an injured person, to rescue a drowning child or otherwise to inconvenience oneself or put oneself at risk for the sake of another. The exceptions occur where there are special relationships between the two persons, like parent and child, teacher and student or doctor and patient. Indeed, certain obligations are imposed on parents with respect to their own children or others in their guardianship, once those children have been born; but, that seems to beg the question.

More pertinent perhaps are various criminal laws that can be applied to the conduct of a mother-to-be that causes the death of the unborn children, conduct like drug use, attempted suicide or reckless driving. See. e.g., Anna North "She had a stillborn baby. Now she's being charged with murder. Her case is part of a nationwide problem, advocates say," *Vox*, November 8, 2019. These laws in some 38 states and in Federal statutes apply to domestic partners and even strangers whose actions cause the death of the fetus. Most of the laws have been enacted in the last 40 years, changing the prior legal standards presumably to provide more protection to pregnant women and their families. See, e.g., Sandra L. Smith, "Fetal Homicide: Woman or Fetus as Victim? A Survey of Current State Approaches and Recommendations for Future State Application," *William & Mary Law Review*, Volume 41, Issue 5, 2000.

However, these laws are now being criticized as part of the attack on all legal restrictions on abortion, because of their possible applicability to such acts. It is anomalous, at least, that a partner's action that causes the loss of an unborn child can be charged as murder whereas action by the mother with the same result is legal.

I think that we need a comprehensive rethinking, and then rewriting, of all of these laws.

One could phrase the question in terms of whether the woman has an obligation to take certain actions or to refrain from certain actions with respect to her own body in order to preserve another life, in this case that of her own unborn child. You might object, "But, abortion is generally an affirmative action designed and intended to end the life of the unborn child". Yet, perhaps, there are principles we can formulate based upon affirmative action versus non-action and on intent. Certainly these concepts are prevalent in our existing laws. Of course, such an approach is certainly different from that advocated by Prof. Arkes.

JUSTIFICATION

It is possible that a relatively broad consensus could be reached on justification, even if one acknowledges that an embryo is a "human life" at a very early stage. The life or health of the mother it is clearly a factor that could constitute "justification". So could be conception occurring through rape or lack of consent. For different reasons, for pregnancy resulting from incest or where there appear to be significant abnormalities. (Prof. Arkes does not find these examples to be "sufficient" justification, but I do not see how he could claim that those conclusions to be "necessary truths".)

I note that "justification" in other contexts does not necessarily turn on blaming the victim. For example, self-defense looks at the reasonable beliefs of the one who killed, not at the blame-worthiness of the one who was killed. And, I believe that some degree of pragmatism is inevitably required in the application of the standards of "justification", whatever they are. For example, it is obvious that any "justifications" would be vacuous if the abortion has to occur within four or six weeks of conception. In addition, the application of the standards must be objectifiable and the outcomes recognizable.

So, it may be that articulation of the "justifications" could satisfy the views of most of the people not on the two extremes.

WHERE TO NOW?

All of this discussion is in a slightly different and more abstract context than the issue that gets the most publicity: whether the majority of voters in any particular jurisdiction can place legal limits on what a woman can do with an unborn fetus or a potential life.

One would think that there should generally be fairly wide discretion left to the political process. We recognize that the community has the right to curb actions contrary to the common interest and to protect its members (especially, those who cannot protect themselves). But, we acknowledge that there are fundamental human rights that cannot be abridged. So, how do we define the rights of the individual in relationship to the rights (and responsibilities) of the community? Maybe a resolution of the tensions between individual and community interests can be fashioned in terms of the concept of "justification" discussed above.

Unfortunately, rational and civil debate has been difficult. Certainly, much harm has been done by the value-burdened language used by both sides in "framing" the issue. And, of course, in the U.S. for some 50 years, the matter of abortion has been largely in the hands of the Federal courts, so most of these questions have been sidelined. If the question is neither when does life begin nor when does life become human, then it must be when is human life to be protected by society. What are the proposed answers to that question?

There simply does not seem to be a principled position among the pro-choice advocates that acknowledges morality. If we were to be given a proposed answer, then we could start an actual dialogue. A consensus might emerge. Note that in Europe, "abortion is legal in most countries, usually with limits that are more strict than America's and generally as a result of democratic choice." The Editorial Board, "Europe's Abortion Lesson: How democracies compromised on the issue after political debate, not judicial fiat," WSJ.com, May 8, 2022.

However, I do think that it is clearly preposterous to assert that a woman's right freely to elect to have an abortion is clear-cut as a moral matter. A moral sensibility requires, at least, the belief that there are some things that matter more than "me". If one acknowledges that moral principles are relevant to human behavior and that human life is "special", then the issue of abortion necessarily involves serious and troubling questions not susceptible to easy answers. I suppose that that assertion itself would offend many pro-choice advocates, a fact that troubles me in and of itself.

Science and Public Policy

Given the nature of scientific models (about which I have written elsewhere), it should be apparent that the application of science to issues of public policy in the messy world in which we live is particularly challenging, involving many potential pitfalls, and is ripe for misunderstandings. This topic was a subject of methodological debates among economists in the mid-twentieth century.

The significance of normative issues

The economist Milton Friedman in his essay on "economics as a positive science" discussed the relationship between scientific knowledge and policy disagreements. "The Methodology of Positive Economics," *Essays in Positive Economics* (1953), pp.3–43. He postulated (admittedly, in an apparently very different era of American history) that many Americans shared common values and that the apparent clashes over policy did not reflect conflicts as deep as they appeared. *Id.*, p.7. He advocated, probably somewhat naively, that efforts should be made to advance economics as a science in order to reduce the disagreements on policy matters.

Indeed, in my undergraduate experience, it appeared that many economists believed that the disputes that arose over policies were mainly the result of lack of clear thinking or a lack of understanding of the science. However, I think that Professor Friedman, like many of the economists I encountered, failed fully to appreciate the normative content of what was thought of as a positive science. He, and others, also probably overestimated the extent of common agreement on the fundamental values that are implicated by political policies.

To many of us in the political middle, the acrimony and blatant bias of much political debate is both striking and distressing. There seems to be an almost utter lack of objective, thoughtful commentary. Everyone has an agenda and many promote theirs with a passion that includes personal animosity toward all opponents. In the face of so much disingenuous self-righteousness, one cannot help but wonder whether there are any roles for logic, facts or unbiased analysis in assessing policy decisions.

CHALLENGES IN APPLYING POSITIVE SCIENCE

A policy question will generally involve (i) a concept or vision of the resulting state of affairs that one would like to achieve through the actions to be taken; (ii) an accurate assessment of the current state of affairs; and (iii) a correct prediction of the likely outcomes of the various potential actions under consideration.

Obviously, people have different values and tastes. Therefore, disagreement can be the result of different views as to which outcomes are more desirable, in light of those values and preferences (moral, aesthetic, or other).

But, there are real problems in making policy choices independent of the differences in values.

We still need to determine accurately the existing state of affairs (sometimes referred to above as the "initial conditions"), before we can predict the likely results of various attempts to effect change. Errors in the assessment of the initial conditions can lead to significant "mistakes" in policy. Even if the policy choices would have been correct if the initial conditions were as they were perceived to be, the choices might have very importantly unexpected consequences because the initial conditions were actually somewhat different. And, even small differences in the initial conditions can lead to large differences in the outcomes. Moreover, differences in good faith predictions of the consequences of potential corrective actions are highly likely, actually inevitable. Such differences can result in widely disparate recommendations as to the steps to be taken.

Indeed, even this description is over-simplified. Many people probably think of the qualitative evaluation of a state of affairs as being measured relative to some principles or values independent of the specific factual situation. if so, part of the policy analysis should take into account the determination of the extent to which the current state of affairs matches or differs from the desired underlying goals and how various potential future states of affairs would do so in comparison. One should even want to consider the potential states of affairs that might result from alternative policies and assess how those results would be graded in terms of the more fundamental, underlying societal objectives.

It is challenging. And, we seem to be getting worse, not better, at applying science to public policy. Micael Crichton identified some potential the causes over 15 years ago:

> "As the twentieth century drew to a close, the connection between hard scientific fact and public policy became increasingly elastic. In part this was possible because of the complacency of the scientific profession; in part because of the lack of good science education among the public; in part, because of the rise of specialized advocacy groups which have been enormously effective in getting publicity and shaping policy; and in great part because of the decline of the media as an independent assessor of fact."

Michael Crichton, "Aliens Cause Global Warming", Caltech Michelin Lecture, January 17, 2003.

POlICY-MAKING AS AN ART

I return to the essay by Professor Friedman with which I started this note. In that essay, Friedman reflected a line of thinking going back at least to John Neville Keynes (the father of the much better known English economist John Maynard Keynes). Keynes had drawn the distinction in 1891 between "...a *positive science* [that] may be defined as a body of systematized knowledge concerning what is [and] a *normative* or *regulative* science [that is] a body of systematized knowledge discussing criteria of what ought to be."

However, Keynes had gone on to draw a third distinction: "an *art* as a system of rules for the attainment of a given end." *The Scope and Method of Political Economy* (1891), pp.34–35. In other words, Keynes believed that policy-making involved more than the normative goals and positive science. This third category--the "art" --was ignored by Friedman in his essay written 60 years later.

The first problem is that most, if not all, of the assessments even of past events or existing facts will be subject to uncertainty, some small and some large in degree. The second problem is that we need to predict future events, as well as the consequences of proposed policies. Both are inherently difficult, if not impossible. For example, most such predictions would be based upon the *ceteris paribus* condition that nothing else changes. Outside of the laboratory, that condition will almost never be satisfied. All kinds of things will change. They always do.

Finally, even if we did have the ability to collect and accurately utilize all of the information providing answers to the relevant questions; the time that would be involved in acquiring that information, processing it, deciding on appropriate polices and then implementing such policies would likely mean that the actions taken will be outdated and overtaken by subsequent events. Similarly, readjustments or reactions to changes are likely to be untimely as well.

The problem of timeliness of information is one of the difficulties that have been identified in debates over the feasibility of centralized economic planning, like in socialism. *See, e.g.,* Friedrich A. Hayek, "The Use of Knowledge in Society," *American Economic Review*, XXXV, No. 4, p. 519, September, 1945.) As a result, it is argued, policies that incorporate automatic or dynamic adjustment mechanisms, where possible, may often be the more effective.

Thus, with respect to every conclusion and prediction we will almost always and necessarily be wrong. The important questions, in each case, will be:

- "How wrong?" and
- "Wrong in which direction?"

The answers to those two questions will also be best guesses, at best.

Finally, all policy choices will have redistributive and re-allocative consequences. They will result in the transfer of wealth and disposable income among persons and groups. They will affect the use of resources as prices of many things adjust to the impact of the policy. They will alter incentives and stimulate some behavior while discouraging other. For example, the availability of government benefits, especially money, seems inevitably to give rise to fraud and corruption., as well as gamesmanship. People are incentivized to seek to gain those benefits. These policies create economic opportunities. And, not socially useful ones.

Such consequences will be both direct and indirect and short-term and long-term. Even after the event, with the benefit of hindsight, economists will find it very difficult to calculate the net effects of all of these consequences. So, it will generally be impossible for anyone to predict these net effects in advance. That is just the way it is.

In the end, effective policy-making will depend upon intuition and instinct, even hunches and guesswork, as well as informed and careful anaysis. That is why it is an art, not a science. And, why experience may be very useful.

Some of the highly-wrought commentary about current policy matters seem to ignore the "art" involved in policy making, attributing differences in judgments to secret or hidden agenda and to selfish motivations. Of course, it would be naïve to suggest that such motivations never exist or that deception and manipulation are not involved in political activities.

Nonetheless, it seems to me that more constructive dialogue might be encouraged by a fuller recognition of the difficulties and uncertainties involved in establishing public policy. Science is never certain, humankind is inherently fallible, and the real world, the one in which we live, is very complex.

A Look at Climate Change and Public Policy

The discussion herein bears only a tenuous relationship to much of what appears in the media as the controversy about climate change. The reason is that most of the media commentary and debate ignores the issues that are central to the determination of sound public policy, while the advocates on all sides promote largely political and emotional agenda advancing personal agendas and interests.

Although, the effects on the environment of gases in the atmosphere have been the subject of scientific inquiry since at least the second half of the nineteenth century,[1] the issue of carbon emissions took on a particular urgency in the twenty-first century. The 2007 report of the United Nation's Intergovernmental Panel on Climate Change ("IPCC") sounded a strident alarm with dire predictions of the likely future consequences of a continuation of our established patterns of energy production and use. Considerable public debate and media coverage has followed.

In early 2014, a committee of the American Association for the Advancement of Science released a report entitled "What We Know." The report set out no new science; instead, it purported to summarize what we already knew and to urge the need for action in language accessible to the lay person. *See, e.g.*, Justin Gillis, "Scientists Sound Alarm on Climate," *The New York Times*, March 18, 2014. The report contained the now often quoted assertion that "about 97% of climate scientists have concluded that human-caused climate change is happening."

As we shall see, that conclusion amounts to very little.

The real questions are: what are the consequences that are likely to occur in the future as a result of continued carbon emissions and what, if anything, can be done about them? It matters very little for issues of policy what the climate would have been like today or in 50 years if we had never generated carbon emissions. Similarly, there is also no real point in bemoaning how much climate change we have or will experience due to carbon emissions in the past. What we want to know specifically is what the future will hold if we do nothing versus what would happen under alternative policies designed to achieve some reasonable and realistic objectives in reducing emissions.

Then, we can have a debate about the potential costs and benefits of the alternatives.

Unfortunately, most of the public debate so far has been framed in terms of conflicts between believers in science and "science-deniers". That dichotomy is both unproductive and misleading. One reason is that, when it comes to policy, science never is and never can be "certain". And, that is certainly the case with respect to the issues that matter. The other important reason is that most really important policy decisions are not about science (as set forth in the prior essay).

Some Background

Natural cycles and chance events

- We know with relative certainty that the Earth has gone through regular periods of warming and cooling over at least the last million years, and we believe (based upon the historical patterns) that the Earth is currently going through one of the periods of warming as part of the normal cycle.
- There is also sound evidence that the more severe of these cycles in the past have had significant impacts on the distribution of life on the planet, on the existing species of animals and on the emergence of new species.
- There is strong evidence that so-called greenhouse gases can contribute to the warming of the Earth independent of the natural cycles. In fact, it appears that greenhouse gases have on at least one occasion resulted in severe climate change and mass extinction (the Permian-Triassic extinction). The emissions in that example, some 250 million years ago, appear to have been the result of volcanic activity.
- A regional mass extinction due to climate change some 160 million years ago appears to have been the result of "polar wander" or shifting tectonic plates. See Maya Wei-Haas, "Earth's odd rotation may solve an ancient climate mystery: A geologic change might have plunged

lush landscapes into arid zones, killing off an array of creatures—and it might happen again one day," *National Geographic*, November 14, 2019.

- "Based on paleoclimate and historical evidence, it is likely that at least one large explosive volcanic eruption would occur during the 21st century. ...Such an eruption would reduce global surface temperature and precipitation, especially over land, for one to three years, alter the global monsoon circulation, modify extreme precipitation and change many [other factors]." Working Group I contribution, *Sixth Assessment Report of the Intergovernmental Panel on Climate Change*, August 7, 2021, at SPM-32 ("AR6").

IMPACT ON HUMANS

- We also have evidence of the significance of the impact of climate change on societies in specific geographical regions. For example, recent research reported in *Geology* has supported the hypothesis that climate change resulting in a prolonged drought was responsible for the disappearance of the large metropolises in Pakistan and India over 4,000 years ago. University of Cambridge, "Decline of Bronze Age 'megacities' linked to climate change," *Research Bulletin*, 27 February 2014. Similarly, Cambridge Gates scholar Mary Beth Day has uncovered evidence that the Cambodian city of Angkor, the largest preindustrial city in the world, collapsed 600 years ago because of climate change. University of Cambridge, "Ancient lessons for a modern challenge," *Research Bulletin*, 20 January 2012.

- Archaeologist Judith Bunbury has been engaged in a long-term study of the impacts of gradual and sudden climate change in Egypt over the past 10,000 years, noting the relocation of populations and economic activity in response. She states: "It's clear from our work in Egypt that there was climate change going on all of the time, and this affected different people in different ways. Resources weren't stationary, so they had to keep moving. ... Some wrote literature about how terrible it was, others just accepted it and moved, and others developed new technologies...." University of Cambridge, "Climate change: it's all happened before...," *Research Bulletin*, 22 October 2013.

- In fact, environmental upheavals may have led to the emergence of *Homo sapiens* as the dominant bipedal species. See Maya Wei-Haas,"Surprising leap in ancient human technology tied to environmental upheaval: Sediment core evidence reveals the critical factors that may have given rise to strikingly complex behaviors some 320,000 years ago, around the time the first members of our species appeared," *National Geographic*, October 21, 2020 ("Scientists have long pointed to changes in climate, such as the onset of wet or dry periods, as the key driving force behind the adaptation of our early ancestors").

IMPACT OF HUMANS

- We know that every year over 200 billion tons of carbon are removed from the atmosphere by growing plants; some 200 billion tons are added back through decomposition, digestion and respiration. Human activity directly adds another 10 billion tons (or 5%). Matt Ridley, *The Rational Optimist*, at 346. Volcanic activity, forest fires and other natural events also contribute emissions to the atmosphere. So, human activity directly makes only a small contribution to the total amount of greenhouse gases in our atmosphere. But, human activity is a net contributor that, at least, to some extent is within our control.
- "[I]n the late 1500s and early 1600s, ...a global drop in surface air temperatures occurred—part of the 'Little Ice Age '—which natural forces can't explain . Quite likely, European expansion in the Americas played a role. With perhaps 90 per cent of the indigenous population eliminated by the effects of conquest and infectious disease, forests reclaimed regions in which terraced agriculture and irrigation had been practised for centuries. In Mesoamerica, Amazonia and the Andes, some 50 million hectares of cultivated land may have reverted to wilderness. Carbon uptake from vegetation increased on a scale sufficient to change the Earth System and bring about a human-driven phase of global cooling." David Graeber and David Wengrow, *The Dawn of Everything: A New History of Humanity* (2021), p.258.
- Since 1850-1900, the rate of carbon emissions has been rising as a result of population and economic growth and that the accumulation of greenhouse gases in the environment has been increasing. We also are relatively certain that this accumulation has had a detectable impact on global temperatures.
- Human impact on the climate includes far more than carbon emissions. "Cities intensify human-induced warming locally, and further urbanization together with more frequent hot extremes will increase the severity of heatwaves (very high confidence). Urbanization also increases mean and heavy precipitation over and/or downwind of cities (medium confidence) and resulting runoff intensity (high confidence). In coastal cities, the combination of more frequent extreme sea level events (due to sea level rise and storm surge) and extreme rainfall/riverflow events will make flooding more probable (high confidence)." AR6, at SPM-33.

- However, not all human activity and emissions cause warming. For example, from the late 19th century to 2010-19, "other human drivers (principally aerosols) contributed a cooling of 0.0°C to 0.8°C, natural drivers changed global surface temperature by −0.1°C to 0.1°C, and internal variability changed it by −0.2°C to 0.2°C. It is ... *extremely likely* that human-caused stratospheric ozone depletion was the main driver of cooling of the lower stratosphere between 1979 and the mid-1990s." AR6, at SPM-6.

And

The effects on climate of the accumulation of carbon in the atmosphere to date will continue for many centuries, even if all further greenhouse emissions were to cease tomorrow. "A thousand years from now—30 human generations—more than half the heat-trapping carbon-dioxide that humanity has pumped into the atmosphere since the beginning of the Industrial Revolution will still be there. Twenty thousand years from now, ... a third of that CO_2 will remain." Jonathan Shaw, "Controlling the Global Thermostat: Coming to terms with climate change's relentless, long-term fallout," *Harvard Magazine*, November-December 2020. Similarly, even with minimal further emissions, "[I]t is virtually certain that global mean sea level will continue to rise over the 21st century. ...In the longer term, sea level is committed to rise for centuries to millennia due to continuing deep ocean warming and ice sheet melt, and will remain elevated for thousands of years ... ." AR6, at SPM-28. "If global net negative CO2 emissions were to be achieved and be sustained, the global CO2-induced surface temperature increase would be gradually reversed but other climate changes would continue in their current direction for decades to millennia ... ." *Id.*, at SPM-39.

Summary

At a minimum, history teaches us that warming and cooling of the planet generally and climate change affecting particular areas are certainly not unnatural nor are the consequences necessarily all bad. We know that climate changes have and will continue to impact human populations. We also know that human activity contributes to climate change. And, finally, we know that global warming as a result of past carbon emissions will continue for the foreseeable future, regardless of our public policies.

What is the relevance of these facts? Not much, except for context. This context should make clear that what is involved in the matter of man-made climate change is not a matter of the fate of Earth. It is a fact that the climate is changing, and always has been. It is also undeniable that human activity (generating greenhouse gases) affects the climate. However, the impacts of human activity on climate are small relative to the climate system as a whole, so the variability attributable to such activities may be insignificant compared to natural variability. See Steven E. Koonin, "'Climate Science Is Not Settled," *The Wall Street Journal*, September 19, 2014.

As always, we are confronting the world we think we know versus the world of he future, about which we can only speculate. The issues are ones of "policy," of the weighing of costs and benefits, of economics and of risk assessment. Thus, it is a matter for serious, reasoned analysis of the facts, the risks, the assumptions and the uncertainties and for dispassionate, critical thinking about our values and priorities.

CLIMATE SCIENCE

We look to climate science to try to predict what the timing and severity of the current warming cycle is likely to be, given the current conditions. In addition, we would like that science to tell us the extent to which human activity is contributing to that change. What we really need to assess is the likely differences it would make if man-made carbon emissions were to be less than what is now expected (based upon current forecasts and known technology) by some potentially feasible amount? So, does climate science have the answers?

THE IPCC ASSESSMENTS

The IPCC Fifth Assessment Report (AR5) was issued in late 2013 and early 2014. (The full-length reports were published by Cambridge University Press.) There are reports from each of three Working Groups (WG1, WG2 and WG3), each of which has a Summary for Policymakers ("SPM"), and a Synthesis Report based upon the work of the three groups. These documents could be seen to represent the state of climate science as of the date of the reports.

The Working Group I part of *The IPCC Sixth Assessment Report* was issued in August 2021 ("AR6").

> "[I]mprovements in observationally based estimates and information from paleoclimate archives provide a comprehensive view of each component of the climate system and its changes to date. **New climate model simulations, new analyses, and methods** combining multiple lines of evidence lead to improved understanding of **human influence** on a wider range of climate variables, including weather and climate extremes. ...The effort was made to estimate temperature change **attributed to total human influence**, changes in well-mixed greenhouse gas concentrations, other human drivers due to aerosols, ozone and land-use change ..., solar and volcanic drivers, and internal climate variability."

AR6, at SPM-5,8 (emphasis added).

The AR6 Summary stresses its efforts to assess all forms of human influence on climate, often referring to "human-induced" changes, and touts the use of "new" models, analyses and methods. Interestingly, the report indicates that but for greenhouse gas emissions, we could be experiencing global cooling. AR6, at SPM-7. Because the full Sixth Assessment Report report is not out yet, I focus below on AR5. [But, I quote from AR6 above. Other excerpts from AR6 are included below, in brackets.]

There are several general observations to be made about AR5. It was less alarmist in many respects than AR4 issued in 2007. It was also somewhat more informative. For example, it provided percentage quantification of the assessments, so one had a firmer idea of what it meant for something to be "likely" or "highly likely". In addition, WG2 concluded that there was little clear evidence of adverse impact upon human health from changes to date, acknowledged that various expected adverse effects were not clearly established by the evidence and forecast that the longer term economic effects of climate change would be only between 0.2 and 2.0% of gross output or income (compared to very much larger previous forecasts). WG2, at SPM-4-8, 19. Repeatedly, the WG2 Report also observed that the adverse impacts of climate change will be felt much more strongly by the poor and by the less developed societies. E.g., *id.* at SPM-6 to 7, 20.

WG1 sets out the evidence concerning the impact of human activity on climate. The key conclusions concern the forecast of climate sensitivity to greenhouse gases, traditionally expressed as the number of degrees of temperature increase caused by a doubling of the concentration of those gases. The sensitivity estimate matters because it is the link between forecasts of the level of future greenhouse emissions and the change in temperature. In other words, one can evaluate different policies in terms of their effects on emissions which can then be translated, using the sensitivity estimate, into expected differences in climate change.

WG1 expressly acknowledged that the 15-year period from 1998 through 2012 showed essentially no warming. It attributed that fact to phenomena—natural variability—that can occur in shorter periods of time but do not alter long term trends. Id. at 5. Yet, based upon that actual experience of the past fifteen years, WG1 lowered the bottom end of the forecast range from 2.0C to 1.5C. The top end, however, remained at 4.5C. WG1, at SPM-16.

The estimates set forth are for equilibrium climate sensitivity ("ECS"), which would be the change that would occur from a doubling of greenhouse gases once all of the adjustments in the climate system had worked themselves out—a period that may be a thousand years. Thus, the ECS could never actually be measured, because other important changes will inevitably occur before equilibrium can be reached. A modified version of ECS looks at a period of 100-150 years.

The "best estimate" of ECS (equilibrium climate sensitivity) went from 3.0C in 1979 (a National Academy of Science report), to 2.5C in AR1 in 1990, back to 3.0C in AR4 (2007). No "best estimate" was given in AR3 (2001) or, now, in AR5 (2014). Lewis and Crok, "A Sensitive Matter," at 19 (Table 1). The reason for the decision in AR5 was set out in footnote 16: "No best estimate for equilibrium climate sensitivity can now be given because of a lack of agreement on values across assessed lines of evidence and studies." What that footnote appears to recognize is that estimates based upon the current observed historical data are not consistent with the forecasts from the climate models being used.

The decision not to publish a "best estimate" has been subject to sharp criticism by some climate scientists and commentators, who assert that the current "best estimate" would be lower than the previous "best estimate" of 3C, perhaps as low as 1.75C. See Nicholas Lewis and Marcel Crok, "A Sensitive Matter: How the IPCC Buried Evidence Showing Good News About Global Warming," The Global Warming Policy Foundation, Report 13, March 5, 2014; Matt Ridley, "Climate Forecast: Muting the Alarm," The Wall Street Journal, March 27, 2014. Such a reduction in the "best estimate" would be a significant development and would undercut many of the policy recommendations of the IPCC. If the current 'best estimate" is less than

2.0C, then the "science" would indicate that the threat is less than previously expected for a given increase in greenhouse gas.

[AR6 reports: "The equilibrium climate sensitivity is an important quantity used to estimate how the climate responds to radiative forcing. ... The AR6 assessed best estimate is 3°C with a *likely* range of 2.5°C to 4°C (*high confidence*), compared to 1.5°C to 4.5°C in AR5, which did not provide a best estimate." AR6, at SPM-14. So, the best estimate is again 3.0C, with an increase in the bottom and a reduction in the top of the range.]

Another relevant measure is transient climate response ("TCR"), which looks at the temperature change when the concentration of gases doubles. The estimate of TCR by WG1 in AR5 is a likely range of 1.0C to 2.5C. Id. at 16. This is the estimate most comparable to historical observations. The estimated range for TCR (transient climate response) has steadily declined from the range of 1.1C to 3.1C set forth in AR3 (2001). See Lewis and Crok, "A Sensitive Matter," at 15.

> *"In the IPCC AR3, it was argued that TCR, rather than ECS, was a more relevant metric of model response to increasing CO2. ...,[T]he overall magnitude of TCR was thought at that time to be more comparable to the time scale and magnitude of the response in the real world over the 21st century. In addition, there were factors that complicated the calculation and interpretation of ECS that were emerging by the late 1990."*

Gerald A. Meehl, Catherine A. Senior, *et al.*, "Context for interpreting equilibrium climate sensitivity and transient climate response from the CMIP6 Earth system models," *Science Advances*, Vol. 6, no. 26, 24 June 2020.

[AR6 "reaffirms with *high confidence* the AR5 finding that there is a near-linear relationship between cumulative anthropogenic CO2 emissions and the global warming they cause. Each 1000 GtCO2 of cumulative CO2 emissions is assessed to *likely* cause a 0.27°C to 0.63°C increase in global surface temperature... . This is a narrower range compared to AR5... ." At SPM-36.]

Of course, greater levels of emission because of greater expected economic activity and/or population growth than previously forecast could create a greater threat despite the possible lower climate sensitivity. And *vice versa*.

Somewhat curiously, climate sensitivity estimates had not changed much since the first estimate in 1979.[2] A major new five-year study by the World Climate Research Program, however, utilizing three independent sources—historical records of temperatures and CO_2 levels, paleoclimate records of prehistoric temperatures (like sediment samples, coral reefs and tree rings), and satellite observations—undertook to narrow the range of climate sensitivity.

The researchers appear to have succeeded:

> *"Very low sensitivities are ruled out by cloud physics and by the understanding from the instrumental and paleo periods. Very high sensitivities would require the understanding of clouds to be wrong in the other direction, aerosols to have a much stronger cooling effect than we thought, and our understanding of paleoclimate changes to be off. ...So* **the likely range for equilibrium climate sensitivity ends up at 2.6-4.1°C,** *with the most likely answer just a hair above 3°C. ... That's considerably narrower than the old 1.5-4.5°C range".*

Scott K. Johnson, "Major study rules out super-high and low climate sensitivity to CO_2: Five-year effort represents important progress on four-decade-old question.," ARSTechnica, July 22, 2020 (emphasis added).

[AR6 claims to find evidence that extreme weather is a result of global warming: "[E]very additional 0.5°C of global warming causes clearly discernible increases in the intensity and frequency of hot extremes, including heatwaves (*very likely*), and heavy precipitation (*high confidence*), as well as agricultural and ecological droughts in some regions (*high confidence*)." AR6, at SMP-19.]

THE MODELS

The assessments described above are in large part based upon models that are vastly more complicated than mere extrapolations from historical evidence. And, there are serious difficulties in reconciling historical evidence with the models.

The starting point in the process is to identify patterns of climate change over some reasonable historical period. Then one can attempt to develop models that would "explain" those changes, that is, models that would generate "predictions" consistent with what happened when applied to past periods. We do not really care very much what the causes were of what happened in the past; however, there is no other established means of predicting what will happen in the future. The assumption is that if a model cannot reconstruct the past, then it seems unlikely that it could accurately predict the future. At the same time, the successful reconstruction of the past (with the benefit of hindsight) is no guarantee of reliability in predicting the future.

Several elaborate models of climate change have been created. At this time, they all seem still to be inadequate for predicting the future, since they have generally appeared to overestimate the change in global temperatures that has occurred over the past 10 to 15 years. *See, e.g.*, Richard McNider and John Christy, "Why Kerrey Is Flat Wrong on Climate Change," *The Wall Street Journal*, February 19, 2014. At the same time, the thawing of the Arctic ice cap seems to be occurring faster than earlier models predicted (although, the ice cap increased in 2013).[3] Efforts to alter the models to capture the Arctic phenomenon have increased the apparent overestimations for the rest of the Earth. *Id.*

Curiously, the deep atmosphere global temperatures (up to 75,000 feet above the surface of the Earth) have not gone up much, but ice in the Northern Hemisphere has been melting rather quickly (while ice in Antarctica has been increasing). *See, e.g.*, Jason Samenow, "Antarctic sea ice hit 35-year record high Saturday," *The Washington Post*, September 23, 2013 (reporting on the new NASA report); Guy Williams, "Why is Antarctic sea ice growing," *Skeptical Science*, 12 December 2013.

Sea ice is the thin layer that forms on the surface of the sea, which is different from glaciers or ice caps. The sea ice does not affect sea levels in the ocean, whereas land ice does. Antarctic land ice is apparently decreasing. *See, e.g., Id.*; "Is Antarctica losing or gaining ice?" *skepticalscience.com.*, 2018.[4] However, the thicker shelf-ice at the edges of the land mass does "slow down the movement of ice flowing from the interior of the continent out to sea. The smaller they are, the less they hold back the flow and the faster ice on land can reach the ocean. That extra ice is what drives increases in sea levels." Daniela Hernandez, "Satellite Study Reveals Wide Scale of Melting Ice Shelves in Antarctica: Results echo previous findings on retreat of continent's ice shelves and go further, enabling better climate models," *WSJ.com*, August 10, 2020.

One might suspect that the explanation of what is happening is, at least, much more complex than is captured in the theory of global warming and, perhaps, that the loss of Arctic ice is due to something other than increased carbon dioxide in the atmosphere. Indeed, there may be such an explanation. "[A] recent paper in the journal *Nature*... argue[s] that CFCs [chlorofluorocarbons] are likely what's caused the Arctic to warm ... faster than the rest of the planet.... . CFCs are, after all, potent greenhouse gases. One shred of optimism: since the phase-out, CFCs have been on the decline, so perhaps this Arctic amplification soon will be, too." Victoria Jaggard, "WHAT'S THE OZONE HOLE GOT TO DO WITH WARMING?" *National Geographic*, February 5, 2020. "Gases that deplete the ozone layer could be responsible for up to half of the effects of climate change observed in the Arctic from 1955 to 2005." Giuliana Viglione, "Ozone-depleting gases might have driven extreme Arctic warming: The far north is heating up twice as fast as the global average," *Nature.com*, 20 January 2020.

Recent results of many of the models are particularly puzzling. "[L]ast year, unnoticed in plain view, some of the models started running very hot. ...The scientists involved couldn't agree on why—or if the results should be trusted." Eric Roston, "Climate Models Are Running Red Hot, and Scientists Don't Know Why: The simulators used to forecast warming have suddenly started giving us less time," *Bloomberg Green*, February 3, 2020. In fact, "one factor might have caused the recent unusual results: clouds. It turns out simulated clouds often cause headaches for climate modelers."

In short, there seem to be many important factors affecting the Earth's climate that the models miss or misapply. And, there are many unknowns:

- Particulates in the atmosphere reflect sunlight back, reducing warming. Changes in activities due to economics or regulations or various natural events, like volcanic eruptions, will affect the amount of particulates present. Similarly. "[c]louds in particular are hugely important. For example, high-altitude, wispy clouds act more like greenhouse gases than shade umbrellas, while low, fluffy clouds can reflect a lot of incoming sunlight back to space." Scott K. Johnson, "Major study rules out super-high and low climate sensitivity to CO_2: Five-year effort represents important progress on four-decade-old question.," *ARSTechnica*, July 22, 2020.[5]

- Our understanding of the impact of changes in the level of greenhouse gases is also hampered by the limitations on our understanding of the oceans and how they will change and thereby affect the climate. We simply have inadequate knowledge of the several other natural feedback systems that can mute or amplify the climate's response. "... [T]he decreasing range of TCR over generations of models, contrasted with the recent increase in range of ECS ..., likely involves processes connected to ocean heat uptake, a better quantification of which

would require improved temperature observations through the full depth of the global ocean ..., as well as increased understanding of various feedbacks in the climate system." Gerald A. Meehl, Catherine A. Senior, *et al*., "Context for interpreting equilibrium climate sensitivity and transient climate response from the CMIP6 Earth system models," *Science Advances*, Vol. 6, no. 26, 24 June 2020 (emphasis added).

- And, there are serious gaps in our understanding of the physical dynamics of glaciers. "Thwaites Glacier [in Western Antartica] is a scientific twofer. ...It contains enough fresh water to raise global sea levels by more than a foot and a half, and it braces the entire West Antarctic Ice Sheet, which could raise sea levels by almost 10 feet if it pooled away. But Thwaites is also ... physically mysterious. In its enormous size and ominous future rest the answers to some of the biggest unresolved questions in climate science.'" Robinson Meyer, "The New Video of One of the Scariest Places on Earth: For the first time, scientists have a clear view of the line where the giant Thwaites Glacier is leaking water into the ocean," *The Atlantic*, January 30, 2020.

The predictions of models are now being treated as empirical data, which they clearly are not. Of course, no empirical data about the future is available. All we have is data about the past and the present. How good is that? Moreover, the results of simulations of the present are now being used to generate simulations of the past. The results of both sets of simulations are used to generate simulations of the future. *See* AR6, *e.g.*, at SPM-3 to 7.

THE DATA

It is clear that there are some pretty serious challenges in measuring climate change for the planet as a whole. Obviously, one can compile data on temperatures, rainfall, and so on for a specific geographical region and can keep track of physical changes in the region that might impact the data. As recent news reports make clear, the short-term weather patterns in various regions will likely vary pretty dramatically. Some areas will be experiencing unusual cold; some, unusual heat; some, floods; some, droughts and so on.

For example, for the year April 2013 to March 2014, England experienced an unusually cold spring; summer came weeks late; the winter was mild but January saw the greatest rainfall on record. Over the same period, California and the American Southwest suffered from a severe and prolonged drought. The American Southeast experienced a snow and ice storm of "historic proportions" in February 2014. New York City and much of the Midwest had an unusually cold winter, with exceptionally large and frequent snow storms. In the summer of 2015, several of the Midwestern States experienced record rain fall, accompanied by highly unusually flooding; France and Italy had record heat waves; and parts of Australia experienced their first ever (recorded) snow fall. Hot or cold years? In 2019, France (and much of Western Europe) experienced a summer of record heat. The American Northwest had an enormous snow storm bringing record snowfall (with accumulations of up to three to four feet) and record low temperatures in September 2019. In early November, much of the United States experienced additional record low temperatures. In late November, the northern half of the country faced an "unprecedented" winter storm disrupting Thanksgiving travel.

NASA has announced that 2019 was the "second hottest year on record. It barely edged out 2016, the previous warmest year. ...And the last decade was the warmest decade." Evan Gough, "According to NASA, 2019 Was the Second Hottest Year on Record," *Universe Today*, January 20, 2020. But, as Gough explains: "The global mean surface temperature is an abstraction in some ways, because the temperature rise is not the same everywhere. In the contiguous 48 US states, the temperature was the 34th highest on record. But there's little comfort in that. The Arctic region is warming about three times faster than the rest of the world."

And, in January 2021:

> *"NASA and the European Union's Copernicus Climate Change Service announced that Earth's average global surface temperature in 2020 tied 2016 as the warmest year on record. Independent studies by the National Oceanic and Atmospheric Administration and a private climate-analysis group called Berkeley Earth found that 2020 was slightly colder than 2016 but warmer than every other year since 1850."*

Robert Lee Holtz, "World's Ice Is Melting Faster Than Ever, Climate Scientists Say: Research shows the Earth lost a sheet of ice 100 meters thick roughly equivalent to the size of the U.K. in recent decades," *WSJ.com*, January 25, 2021.

So, how, in fact, does one collect data on the planet as a whole? One would probably say take measurements in many places all around world, using consistent methodology and standardized equipment. Of course, you need to collect the same data year after year for many years, decades or even centuries. (It is obviously too late to go back to do it or to redo it.) Then, climate scientists have to develop definitions to be applied to all of the data from various regions (how to combine and weigh the disparate results) to determine whether in the aggregate there has been global warming (as so defined). Yet, there is still uncertainty.

For example, one would presumably determine changes in the temperature of the oceans by using multiple thermometers to take water temperatures in many, many locations. That is essentially what scientists have done (but, overall, there have not been consistent measurements collected over decades).

Indeed, the most common method of measurement has been by sailors taking buckets full of sea water and taking their "temperature". See, e.g., Rebecca Hersher, "How Much Hotter Are The Oceans? The Answer Begins With A Bucket," NPR, August 19, 2019. Among other problems, the temperature of the water changes quickly after collection, depending upon the bucket size and the air temperature.

A 2018 study reports:

> "... that between 1991 and 2016 the oceans warmed an average of 60 percent more per year than the [IPCC] panel's official estimates. [H]owever, t]he researchers used **a new approach that derived ocean temperatures by measuring the levels of carbon dioxide and oxygen in the atmosphere**. Those gases dissolve in ocean waters, but the amount the ocean can hold depends on its temperature."

Kendra Pierre-Louis, "Taking the Oceans' Temperature, Scientists Find Unexpected Heat," NYTimes.com., October 31, 2018 (emphasis added).

Which is more accurate, the direct measurements or the measurements by inference from the atmosphere? Are either reasonably correct? Of course, the methodological problems are eased somewhat by the fact that one need only to determine the changes over time not the absolute temperature levels.

But, there are still issues. For example, some climate scientists in 2015 concluded that the apparent slow-down in global warning was the result of errors made in the way global warming was measured—when the data is "corrected", the warming trend reappears. See, e.g., Justin Gillis, "Global Warming 'Hiatus' Challenged by NOAA Research," *The New York Times*, June 4, 2015 (the data issues focus on the measurement of the temperature of seawater by sailors collecting buckets of sea water and measuring the temperature of the water in the buckets with thermometers). Other climate scientists have challenged these tentative conclusions. It also seems that the revisions to the data proposed significantly reduce the apparent warming since 1880, while also reducing the amount by which the warning seems to have slowed down in the last 15 years. *Id.*

Our models necessarily take data from the past (which is all that we have) and project that data into the future. The assumption (almost certainly wrong) is that the future will be like the past. Thomas Malthus, in the 18th century, predicted the continual return of mankind to a mere subsistence level of existence, because population growth was exponential while agricultural productivity growth was arithmetic. In the early 1970s, we supposedly faced a catastrophic worldwide population explosion, because of the steady exponential growth rate of the world's population. In both cases, the mathematics were impeccable, but the assumptions about the facts (in the future) were simply wrong. *See, e.g., id. See also*, Laurence B. Siegel, *Fewer, Richer, Greener: Prospects for Humanity in an Age of Abundance* (2020) (the title of this book, like its organization, is a bit misleading: the evidence presented suggests that "richer" leads to "fewer" and then, eventually, to "greener").

Eric Roston, in the article cited above, notes: "To a degree, every scientist suspects their model is wrong. There's even an aphorism about this: 'All models are wrong, but some are useful.'" Michael Crichton, in a speech 15 years ago, reviewed numerous examples of alarmist predictions by scientists during the twentieth century that turned out to be false (such as the "nuclear winter", the food shortage and the population explosion), commenting:

> "*I have to say* **the arrogance of the model-makers is breathtaking**. *There have been, in every century, scientists who say they know it all. Since climate may be a chaotic system ... these predictions are inherently doubtful, to be polite. ...[E]ven if the models get the science spot-on, they can never get the sociology.* **To predict anything about the world a hundred years from now is simply absurd.** *...You tell me you can predict the world of 2100. Tell me it's even worth thinking about.* **Our models just carry the present into the future. They're bound to be wrong.** *Everybody who gives a moment's thought knows it.*"

"Aliens Cause Global Warming", *Caltech Michelin Lecture*, January 17, 2003 (emphasis added).

Not convinced? Just look at the dramatic yet unpredictable changes between 1920 and 2020, or 1820 and 1920, or even 1720 and 1820. And, of course, as most of us are keenly aware, the pace of change has been increasing "exponentially" (whatever that means). In the end, we might question the actual usefulness of computer models attempting to forecast very far into the future.

Some examples of the challenges

One example

Let's take a conceptually simple example, relatively free of the problems of technological change and other issues of forecasting: What is the net relationship between trees (and plants generally) and climate change?

Trees absorb carbon from the atmosphere as they grow, but they release carbon when they die and decompose (or are burned). Warming temperatures and more CO_2 in the atmosphere promote tree growth, causing the trees to grow faster. Faster growth means greater carbon absorption. But, faster growth may also mean shorter lives for the trees, resulting in faster release of carbon. *See* University of Cambridge, "Amount of carbon stored in forests reduced as climate warms," *Research*, 15 May 2019 ("As the Earth's climate continues to warm, tree growth will continue to accelerate, but the length of time that trees store carbon, the so-called carbon residence time, will diminish"). So, older, slower growing trees generally live longer, but they also absorb less carbon per year. Separately, the green leaves of trees absorb more of the Sun's heat than do other, lighter ground cover (like snow, especially), which reflects more sunlight. *See* Gabriel Popkin, "How much can forests fight climate change?" *Nature*, 15 January 2019. Well, so what is the net impact of trees?

There are similar issues about the assumed rate of absorption of carbon from the atmosphere by plants generally. Growing plants pull from the atmosphere tremendous quantities of carbon (while rotting plants return the carbon). Thus, the rate of deforestation and other reductions or increases in the quantities of plant life are relevant to the results obtained from the models. At the same time, there is some expectation that the increasing levels of carbon dioxide and higher temperatures will spur plant growth in the near term. But, increasing prevalence of drought conditions may reduce the amount of vegetation, reducing the capability to absorb carbon and even increasing the rate of release of carbon back into the atmosphere. There is also the possibility that at some point, higher temperatures will result in the saturation of the aggregate ability of plants to absorb additional carbon, which could result in a sudden surge in greenhouse gases and more rapid climate change. *See* University of Cambridge, "4 degree temperature rise will end vegetation 'carbon sink,'" *Research*, 17 December 2013.

Then, there are also questions about other impacts on the environment of plant growth stimulated by rising levels of CO_2, such as on the availability of water for human use. *See* Stephen Leahy, "Thirsty future ahead as climate change explodes plant growth: Rising CO_2 levels and a warmer earth means plants will grow bigger and have longer to suck the land dry. That's bad news for human water supplies," *National Geographic*, November 4, 2019. Consider this explanation given by Leahy:

> *"Climate change affects the growth of plants in three ways. First, as CO_2 levels increase, plants need less water to do photosynthesis. This well-documented effect was long thought to mean that there would be more fresh water available in soils and streams. But a second effect counters that: A warming world means longer and warmer growing seasons, which gives plants more time to grow and consume water, drying the land. ...[The] third effect: As CO_2 levels rise, it amps up photosynthesis. Plants in this hotter, CO_2-rich environment grow bigger, with more leaves. That means when it rains there will be far more wet leaves creating more surface area for more evaporation to occur."*

So, more CO_2 means less water use per plant. But, more CO_2 also means more and bigger plants, using more water. And, more and bigger leaves means more evaporation. But, more plant growth means more CO_2 pulled from the atmosphere. Yet, more leaf coverage means more heat absorption and more evaporation!

Pretty complicated.

Two other examples

Bacteria and other micro-organisms are among the tiny particles that seed the formation of crystalline structuring of water that create snowflakes and ice crystals as the first stage in most rainfall, as well as all snow and hail. Bacteria that are able to withstand the intense ultraviolet light and lack of nutrients in the upper atmosphere could travel throughout the world in airborne colonies. Presumably, these bacteria affect weather patterns, so the changing of a regional microbiome (for example, through agriculture) or changes in particular microbiomes that occur as a result of climate change may affect the weather in such regions or elsewhere. Ferris Jabr, "It's Buggy Out There," *The New York Times Magazine*, February 13, 2015. How does one model this relationship?

Look at the relationship between methane leaks and microbes.

> *"The first active leak of methane from the sea floor in Antarctica has been revealed by scientists. The researchers also found microbes that normally consume the potent greenhouse gas before it reaches the atmosphere had only arrived in small numbers after five years, allowing the gas to escape. …The research also has significance for climate models, which currently do not account for a delay in the microbial consumption of escaping methane."*

Damian Carrington, "First active leak of sea-bed methane discovered in Antarctica," *The Guardian*, 21 July 2020.[7]

A SUMMARY COMMENT

Steven Koonin observes that the important questions have not been answered by science to date and the widespread belief that climate science is settled "distorts our public and policy debates" and "has inhibited the scientific and policy discussions that we need to have." "Climate Science Is Not Settled," *The Wall Street Journal*, September 19, 2014. The simple, stark fact is that "climate science … is not yet mature enough to usefully answer the difficult and important questions being asked of it." *Id.*

THE BIG QUESTIONS

Let us assume that we could predict with reasonable reliability the causes and processes of climate change under current conditions. Several important questions still arise:

- First, absent some change from the status quo, what are the conditions that are likely to exist at various times in the future? For example, what daily and seasonal temperatures do we predict? What, if any changes, in acidity will occur? What will the pattern of rainfall be? Will there be flooding (for example, from rising sea levels)?
- Second, taking some reasonable estimate of what it might be possible to change about the current trends, such as reductions in the aggre-

gate expected future amount of greenhouse gases in the atmosphere, what are the conditions that would be likely to exist at the same times in the future?
- Third, what are likely to be the impacts on environment, agriculture, existing species of plants and animals, man-made infrastructure and facilities of both sets of future conditions (under the first scenario and under the second scenario)?
- Finally, what is the array of feasible policy actions that could be effectively implemented, especially on a global basis?

Then, there are related big questions. I discuss six below.

But, first, note: the feared adverse consequences simply may not be avoidable merely by curtailing future carbon emissions: "[T]emperatures will continue to increase progressively... Unless the process can be reversed—not just slowed—the globally transformative effects of human-induced warming will thus extend across a geological time scale that has come to be known among scientists as the *anthropocene...* ." Jonathan Shaw, "Controlling the Global Thermostat: Coming to terms with climate change's relentless, long-term fallout," *Harvard Magazine*, November-December 2020. So, it may be that engineered projects to recapture carbon and to alter the environmental dynamics are the only hope. See, e.g., *id.*; Daniel Schrag and David Keith, "Can Solar Geoengineering Help Fight Climate Change?" *Harvard Magazine*, Podcast, October 16, 2020.

And, a comment about recent (2020) events. Interestingly, in the second quarter of 2020, we experienced a natural (unplanned and unintentional) experiment. A dramatic decrease in global economic activity due to a pandemic has resulted in a decrease in carbon emissions, a reduction in pollution, clearer skies, cleaner water, the presence of fish (and jellyfish) in Venetian canals, the visibility of the Himalayas from the Indian state of Punjab, and much less road congestion. See, e.g., "Coronavirus: Air pollution and CO_2 fall rapidly as virus spreads," BBC.com, 19 March 2020; "'We can see the Himalayas for the first time in 30 years' – from India to Venice, the beautiful side effects of the coronavirus pandemic," *The Telegraph*, 9 April 2020; Jim Carlton, "Coronavirus Offers a Clear View of What Causes Air Pollution," WSJ.com, May 3, 2020 ("With factories and vehicles idle, nitrogen dioxide levels hit lows not seen since the early 20th century; 'We didn't know was how significantly it could drop'"). We also are seeing the takeover of National Parks (and even city streets) by native wildlife. Nature is reasserting itself much faster than we ever would have expected. See, e.g., "7 ways the earth has gotten better since the coronavirus shutdown," *The Philadelphia Inquirer*, April 22, 2020. We may have the unique opportunity actually to examine the environmental consequences of certain changes in our economies and our behavior. This event may also give us insights into the human costs of various such changes.

Now, the related over-arching questions.

1. WHERE WILL THE PREDICTED NEGATIVE IMPACTS MOST LIKELY OCCUR?

What would seem to matter as far as public policy is what will be happening in specific geographical regions, not mere changes in some global average. So, we need to answer the above questions with respect to specific geographic regions, not with global averages. Clearly, these issues have meaning only in a local context. We would want not only to identify the impacts but also to place values or costs on them or, at least, on the differentials identified. Thus, the identification of the specific regions to be affected is crucial. Thus, the actual analysis will be even more complex than the public debate suggests.

One question is what impact global warming is having and will have on regional weather patterns. In 2012, National Geographic featured on its cover a story with the question "What's Up With The Weather?" Accompanying the customary spectacular photographs, the author described the apparent dramatic increase in extreme weather events during the twenty-first century. They ranged from "Record Floods" to "Endless Drought", from "Summer in March" to "Snowmageddon." Peter Miller, "Weather Gone Wild," *National Geographic*, September 2012, at 30-65. Global warming seems to have increased the amount of water evaporation which, in turn, contributes to making the normal weather patterns more extreme. Of course, there may be other explanations.

Some of the rather severe recent weather patterns in the United Kingdom and the United States seem to be as a result of changes in the path of the jet stream possibly caused by climate change. It has been proposed that the warming trend in the arctic region has altered the relationships in atmospheric temperatures around the Northern Hemisphere so as to allow the jet stream to wander or meander, bringing unusual and potentially prolonged weather patterns. See, e.g., Pallab Ghosh, "Wavier jet stream 'may drive weather shift,' BBC News, Science & Environment, 15 February 2014. The current drought in California, however, may just be a typical cyclical phenomenon unrelated to climate change. See Justin Gillis, "Science Linking Drought to Global Warming Remains Matter of Dispute," *The New York Times*, February 16, 2014 (reporting that there is no consensus among scientists nor any definitive evidence linking the drought to global warming).

For the east coast of the United States and the Carribean, there are significant questions about the relationship between climate change and hurricanes.

> "[E]xperts say it has been challenging to draw conclusions with limited data. While many scientists agree that global warming is responsible **for more rainfall** in these storms, and has **no effect on storm frequency**, there is no consensus on a link between warming and the storm intensification and wind strength."

Denise Chow and Andrew Williams, "This year's Atlantic hurricane season was worse than normal, but it wasn't nearly as destructive as much of the last 10 years: While scientists say global warming is to blame for wetter storms, no consensus exists for such a link to storm strength," NBC News, December 10, 2019 (emphasis added).[6]

The point of importance here is simply that the particular effects of climate change in different areas are likely to be quite different and difficult to forecast. In short, the nature and amount of the expected impact of global climate change varies by region, as do the likely costs and benefits of that change. Yet, the ability of climate science to predict regional impacts is quite limited.

2. COULD EXPECTED DAMAGE FROM THE PREDICTED NEGATIVE IMPACTS BE AMELIORATED?

With respect to each of the impacts identified, are there other steps that could be taken to ameliorate the negative effects? If so, what would be the costs of those steps? These analyses will necessarily be focused on bits and pieces.

Certainly, one should want to assess the potential costs of means of ameliorating or avoiding the costs of climate change as an alternative to trying to avoid the change itself. The costs of the policies of intervention would be avoided, and some significant portions of the predicted damage of the climate change could be minimized. I suspect that projects that could help cope with the changing conditions could be achieved at relatively reasonable cost and utilizing already available or easily realized technology.

It has been estimated that the number and costs of major weather disasters for the period 1996-2011 was almost twice that of the period 1980-96, in standardized dollars. Peter Miller, "Weather Gone Wild," *National Geographic*, September 2012, at 54-5. The author observes, however, that the numbers reflect the fact that "more people are located in harm's way." Greater concentrations of people, more buildings and, often, more expensive buildings are being located in highly vulnerable places (like the coastlines). "Instead of defending themselves against climate change, many communities appear to be leading with their chin." *Id.* at 52. Similarly, Phil Klotzbach, of Colorado State University, has been quoted as saying: "even if you think climate change is a hoax, hurricanes are going to do more damage because we've built up coastlines and so there are more people in harm's way." Chow and Williams, "This year's Atlantic hurricane season was worse than normal, but it wasn't nearly as destructive as much of the last 10 years," NBC *News*, December 10, 2019.

One could adopt zoning and building regulations that reduce the future risks of climate change. Similarly, if one predicts that a current residential area would be flooded by rising sea levels, destroying homes for hundreds or thousands of families, it would be worth investigating what the feasibility and cost would be of constructing dykes, sea walls and drainage systems sufficient to preserve those homes. It would also be worth estimating what it would cost to relocate those families, in human terms as well as in material resources.

There are a host of possible adjustments that can (and will) be made. For example, "'[a]s the climate changes, you can either move the farm or you can change the plant. It's easier to change the plant,' says Hanna Neuschwander, communications director at World Coffee Research, a nonprofit research firm that is coordinating scientists' efforts to engineer coffee varieties that can thrive in higher temperatures." Patience Haggin, "What Rising Temperatures Mean for Coffee-Bean Farmers: As rising temperatures threaten to reduce the area in the tropics suitable for growing coffee, scientists work to engineer more resilient coffee plants," *WSJ.com*, October 9, 2019.

Indeed, it would seem to be sensible to investigate the means of reducing the impact of climate change as a first step; if, for no other reason, than the likelihood that climate change will be experienced to some significant degree regardless of any efforts made to reduce greenhouse gases. Indeed, even to the extent that the policies can only delay and not avoid the damage, these steps may be particularly significant.

3. WHAT ARE THE LIKELY EFFECTS OF TECHNOLOGICAL CHANGE ON THE PREDICTIONS?

While it may be interesting to be able to predict what the future would be if nothing changes, the one thing we know for certain is that there will be change, and change in many things. For example, is it likely that new non-carbon or low-carbon sources of energy will be developed over the next 25 or 50 years?

The answer, based upon history, would have to be yes.

The real issues have to do with the costs and the scalability of those technologies. Will they become economic, and will they be capable of delivering some significant portion of the world's emery needs? Again, history suggests that the most likely answer to both questions is yes. See Matt Ridley, *The Rational Optimist*, at 139-56, 191-200, 217-43 (Ridley chronicles several of the truly spectacular successes of technology, combined with division of labor, specialization and trade, in expanding the world's food supply and its industrial production, creating a far, far wealthier and healthier human population than most people could imagine even in the nineteenth century). Dramatic improvements in battery technology are already being realized. See, e.g., Chris Hall, "Future batteries, coming soon: Charge in seconds, last months and power over the air," *Pocket-lint.com*, 7 October 2020.

> *"The battery boom could erode demand for crude oil and byproducts such as gasoline—as well as for natural gas, which is primarily used in power plants. While mining materials and manufacturing batteries produces some greenhouse gas emissions, analysts believe shifting to batteries in the auto and energy sectors would reduce emissions overall, boosting efforts to tackle climate change".*

Russell Gold and Ben Foldy, "The Battery Is Ready to Power the World: After a decade of rapidly falling costs, the rechargeable lithium-ion battery is poised to disrupt industries," *WSJ.com*, February 5, 2021.

Renewable energy sources have become cost-effective and often cheaper than traditional sources. See, e.g., Amory B. Lovins and M. V. Ramana, "Three Myths About Renewable Energy and the Grid, Debunked," *Yale Environment* 360, December 9, 2021.

And, here is another example. "This planet is home to about 1.5 billion cows, which collectively produce a lot of gas. In fact, they create more greenhouse gas emissions than planes, trains and automobiles combined."

"Adding Red Seaweed To Cow Feed Could Cut Bovine Flatulence," NPR (WAMU 88.5), December 2, 2020. Of particular concern is the production of methane (CH_4) by cows and sheep during digestion, since methane has 28 times the greenhouse effect of carbon dioxide. Robert Talbot, "Methane Is A Powerful Greenhouse Gas, But Where Does It Come From?" *Forbes*, September 29, 2017 (The increase in methane is not the result of increased oil and gas production; "it appears that increasing agriculture and human population is a more likely scenario"). But, "[r]esearch shows that a specific type of seaweed can cut cows' methane production by up to 98%." *Id.*

So, we can stop eating beef and cheese, drinking milk and wearing wool and leather or, perhaps, we could starting feeding cows (and sheep) some tropical red seaweed (specifically, A*sparagopsis taxiformis*). Small amounts of this seaweed also improve the digestive process leading to healthier cows. Commercial production of the product is already beginning. See Jeff Kart, "Hawaiian Seaweed Makes Cows 90% Less Gassy-And That's Good For Climate Change," *Forbes.com*, November 21, 2020.

In short, the desired benefits might be much more easily achieved through innovation than through coercive policies.

4. What are the likely impacts of cultural change on the predictions?

Separately, we should ask what relevant changes in societal values and practices will occur over time as more societies become richer? They will almost certainly occur. The issues are what and when?

For example, it is likely that carbon emissions will follow the pattern of the population explosion, viewed as a major threat in 1970–the mathematics of exponential growth were beyond dispute, but the assumptions about the world were wrong. We should expect that carbon emissions will continue to fall in the developed countries and then do so elsewhere as the less developed countries become more prosperous. See, *e.g.*, Laurence B. Siegel, *Fewer, Richer, Greener* (2020).[8] And, "[t]here are other ways that economic development supports the environment. ...[I]f economic development spreads the blessings of greater freedom and greater education to more of the world, popular demands for cleaner air, cleaner water and the protection of nature will only grow." *Id.*

In the meantime, the less developed countries will need cheap energy (fossil fuels) to become prosperous. What is the timing of this likely development?

5. What are the likely costs (and benefits) of immediate corrective actions?

If we had good models of climate change and reasonable predictions of technological developments, we could, in theory, assess the potential costs to the Earth of a continuation of man's current behavior relative to what would be likely to occur if the growth of such emissions were curtailed. We could then compare those avoidable costs (*i.e.*, benefits) with the estimated costs of programs that would reduce the emissions.

The questions we would be trying to answer are: What would the world be like in 100 years if we do nothing? What would it be like if various possible changes were made? Are the differences resulting from the policy changes likely to be permanent or only temporary? That is, would our efforts avoid or merely delay the occurrence of the consequences? And, what would be the costs to society of making those various changes? With the answers to these questions, one could have a sensible debate about what to do.

It is important to remember that the carbon emissions at issue are largely the result of activities that have provided great benefits to large portions (but not all) of world's population in the form of economic prosperity and material wellbeing. Changes in those activities as a result of policy-making will have costs in the form of the losses of benefits that would otherwise be enjoyed. In addition, of course, there will be the more direct costs of the policies as well. Moreover, governmental regulation carries substantial transaction costs beyond the impact of the rules themselves, much in terms of bureaucratic overhead, inevitable mistakes in policy implementation and, unfortunately, corruption.

Furthermore, alternatives to fossil fuels have costs as well, in terms of the resources used, other impacts on the environment and the possible disruptions of implementation. *See, e.g.*, Charlie McGee, "Wood Pellets Draw Fire as Alternative to Coal: A lawsuit says European policy on using pellets will increase greenhouse-gas emissions; 'burning gas would release far less carbon dioxide,' expert says," *WSJ.com*, Aug. 7, 2019; Mark P. Mills," If You Want 'Renewable Energy,' Get Ready to Dig: Building one wind turbine requires 900 tons of steel, 2,500 tons of concrete and 45 tons of plastic," *WSJ.com*, August 5, 2019; Russel Gold, "Building the Wind Turbines Was Easy. The Hard Part Was Plugging Them In," *WSJ.com*, June 22, 2019 ("We have 21st-century technology to produce the power, but we still have a 20th-century power grid that can't move it from the windy and sunny parts of the country to the urban markets. The American power grid isn't set up for it"); Chris Martin, "Wind Turbine Blades Can't Be Recycled, So

They're Piling Up in Landfills: Companies are searching for ways to deal with the tens of thousands of blades that have reached the end of their lives," *Bloomberg Green*, February 5, 2020.

Indeed, in 2021, the International Energy Agency ("IEA") issued a report on the process of transition to "green" energy, warning that it might not be attainable:

> *"An energy system powered by clean energy technologies differs profoundly from one fuelled by traditional hydrocarbon resources. Solar photovoltaic (PV) plants, wind farms and electric vehicles (EVs) generally require more minerals to build than their fossil fuel-based counterparts. A typical electric car requires six times the mineral inputs of a conventional car and an onshore wind plant requires nine times more mineral resources than a gas-fired plant. ...The prospect of a rapid rise in demand for critical minerals – in most cases well above anything seen previously – poses* **huge questions about the availability and reliability of supply**.*"*

"The Role of Critical Minerals in Clean Energy Transitions: Part of World Energy Outlook," IEA *Flagship Report*, May 2021, Executive Summary (emphasis added).

Efforts to achieve the transition will result in an increase in greenhouse emissions for years. The report also identifies additional serious challenges to the transition in terms of adverse environmental impact and energy security, further warning: "Tackling the environmental and social impacts of mineral developments will be essential, including the emissions associated with mining and processing, risks arising from inadequate waste and water management, and impacts from inadequate worker safety, human rights abuses (such as child labour) and corruption." *Id.*

The costs and benefits will not all be readily measurable dollar terms. One would need to find a way to value benefits such as the preservation of potentially endangered species, the protection of existing communities, and the avoidance of adverse impacts on life style. One would also need to find a means of valuing the costs of reduced economic growth and restrictions on various amenities that we, especially in the developed world, currently take for granted.

6. Who will bear the costs (or enjoy the benefits) of any such corrective actions?

In evaluating alternative policy responses, there is necessarily more involved than just comparing the total estimated costs with the total estimated benefits. The costs and benefits would not be shared equally across the world's population. Indeed, some of the more substantial costs in terms of reduced economic activity would fall primarily upon the less developed and less wealthy societies.

It is, perhaps, ironic that the IPCC reports stress the prediction that the adverse impacts of climate change would fall more heavily on the poor and on the less developed societies. Ironic because, at the same time, it seems likely that the costs of policies to mitigate greenhouse emissions would also fall disproportionately on the same constituencies. (Cheap energy and lavish exploitation of raw materials have been important sources of the rapid industrialization of the developed world.) And, many of the benefits of such policies (especially the intangible ones) would fall disproportionately on the wealthier societies.

How does one account for the disparate impacts of a policy that reduces carbon emissions? Can these impacts be offset by mere transfer payments?

Also, it should not be surprising that it appears that climate change ranks very low on the lists of concerns of the world's poorest inhabitants. Food, shelter, sanitation, cheap energy, medical care, education, jobs and numerous other basics of a healthy and happy life are far more urgent and significant to those who do not have those necessities. See, e.g., Bjorn Lomborg, "This Child Doesn't Need a Solar Panel," *The Wall Street Journal*, October 21, 2015 (referencing a United Nations survey of over 8 million people in which those from the poorest countries ranked action on climate change last among a list of 16 public policy goals.)

That is not to say that policies to address climate change necessarily come at the cost of assistance to those suffering from other, more immediate challenges, but resources are limited and some of the policy remedies for climate change do have implications for other aspects of people's lives.

So...?

Obviously, the answers to these questions would be only a part of a bigger, interrelated calculation that would attempt to accumulate the costs and benefits of alternative policy approaches. And, any global policy would also need to deal with the serious issue of the distribution of the resulting costs and benefits among the world's current and future generations.

However, Matt Ridley sets forth his conclusions as follows:

> "I find ... the probability of rapid and severe climate change is small; the probability of net harm from the most likely climate change is small; the probability that no adaptation will occur is small; and the probability of no new low-carbon energy technologies emerging in the long run is small. Multiply those small probabilities together and the probability of a prosperous twenty-first century is therefore by definition large. ... [It is] **very probable that the world will be a better place in 2100 than it is today.**"

The Rational Optimist, at 347 (emphasis added).

Conclusions?

Reality and Global Politics

In the end, we need to face reality. The fact is that we will never be able actually to obtain the answers to any, let alone all, of these questions. At best we will have approximate, incomplete and dated answers. And, we will have to deal with people and nations.

Underlying any attempt to find solutions will be the ugly face of uncertainty. All of our predictions about the process of climate change and of the consequences of every action that might be taken will be necessarily be subject to uncertainty to varying (but probably unknown) degrees. The point is that all policies "carry costs, risks and questions of effectiveness"; moreover, "nonscientific factors inevitably enter the decision. These include our tolerance for risk and the priorities that we assign to economic development, poverty reduction, environmental quality, and intergenerational and geographical equity." Koonin, "Climate Science Is Not Settled," The Wall Street Journal, September 19, 2014.

It is important to note that the discussion set out above certainly does not, in my view, demonstrate that human-induced climate change is not real nor that it is not a threat. The arguments here concern the types of actions that could rationally and reasonably be taken in response to what concededly is a problem. The point is that many of the proposed cures are likely worse than the disease or will, on balance, make the world worse off than it would be if nothing were done. We are talking about public policy after all. Moreover, we may have already passed the "tipping point"—the point of no return, absent technology to reverse the accumulation of greenhouse gases (carbon recapture).

In addition, we will always need carefully to assess the feasibility and achievability of any proposed solution or means of reducing emissions. The challenge is especially acute because the causes and sources of emissions are global. The action of one nation is unlikely to make a difference, unless it becomes an example followed by many others. How can we assure the serious commitment of China, now the largest source of carbon emissions by far? Or, of India and Russia, numbers three and four?

The 2019 climate conference lasted two weeks yet produced no agreements on actions. *See, e.g.,* Brady Dennis and Chico Harlan, "U.N. climate talks end with hard feelings, few results and new doubts about global unity," *The Washington Post,* December 15, 2019 ("a handful of higher-emitting countries squared off against smaller, more vulnerable countries. Negotiators were at loggerheads while crafting rules around a fair and transparent global carbon trading system, and they pushed the issue to next year. Fights also dragged on about how to provide funding to poorer nations already coping with rising seas, crippling droughts and other consequences of climate change"). Other Issues in contention include the allocation of the costs among the more developed and less developed countries. In addition, many countries face other pressing concerns.[9]

SUBSIDIES

I would eliminate the various subsidies for alternative fuels and for electric vehicles (mainly enjoyed by the relatively wealthy and the manufacturers). Government subsidies generally provide very poor "bang for the buck." And, they almost always result in waste and misallocations of resources. For example, subsidies for the purchase of EVs largely drive up the prices charged for the EVs relative to gasoline powered vehicles. (Just like university tuition responding to subsidized student loans and health insurance premiums soaring under Obamacare.) Also, as with most government payments, subsidies attract corruption and fraud. The larger the payments, the greater the attraction. The main advantage of subsidies is that they are politically much easier to enact. For the average voter, subsidies just mean transfers from one group of wealthy people to another.

Some new models support a negative view of subsidies. For example:

"Clean energy subsidies have two countervailing effects. First, they make clean energy less expensive, thereby creating incentives for agents to produce energy with clean sources. ... Second, clean energy subsidies reduce the price of the energy composite [increasing energy usage]. This additional effect is also governed by the share of clean energy in the energy composite... . [I[n the quantitative model we have put forward, these two effects roughly cancel out. Subsidies as large as 75% yield only a minuscule reduction in CO_2 emission and temperatures. We conclude that clean energy subsidies are not an effective way to combat global warming."

José-Luis Cruz and Esteban Rossi-Hansberg, "The Economic Geography of Global Warming," NBER Working Paper No. 28466, February 2021 (emphasis added).

A Carbon Tax

Nonetheless, some action seems like a prudent precautionary measure, given the uncertainty of the predictions on all fronts. "... [I]t's entirely possible to envision climate-related policies that would meet a cost-benefit test. Investing in basic science and research is almost always high-return." Holman W. Jenkins, Jr., "How Greens Humiliate Themselves," *The Wall Street Journal*, Oct. 30, 2018. Personally, like Holman Jenkins of the *Wall Street Journal*, I favor taxes on fossil fuels and on activities that generate greenhouse gases, *i.e.*, a "carbon tax". Perhaps, also a "methane tax" on livestock (increasing the cost of meat) and on natural gas production (based upon estimated leakage).

I would do so on the traditional economic theory of externalities. Certain activities have known and identifiable (but not necessarily quantifiable) adverse effects on others. Where those effects are born by society generally, it is reasonable to impose a fee on the activities in question in order to shift some of those burdens to those receiving the benefits, in effect bringing those costs into the price paid. The fees would generate revenue that could be used to compensate society for the burdens being imposed (if not "revenue-neutral"). And, the cost of fossil fuels to its users would better reflect the costs to society.

Of course, those fees are also very likely to cause a reduction in the activities on which the fee is imposed, by making them more expensive relative to alternatives. The tax would create economic opportunities in achieving reductions of energy use, in general, and the use of fossil fuels, in particular. This approach has the advantage of relying on the market to make continuous, dynamic adjustments to changing circumstances and of providing incentives for corrective behavior.

> *"In sum, the main effect of a carbon tax is to delay dirty energy consumption, by spreading its use over time; less current consumption but more future consumption. The more protracted path for CO2 emissions has stark implications for the evolution of global temperatures: It flattens the temperature curve. A carbon tax of 200% leads to an evolution of average global temperatures that is as much as 4 °C lower in the first half of the 22nd century... ."*

José-Luis Cruz and Esteban Rossi-Hansberg, "The Economic Geography of Global Warming," NBER Working Paper No. 28466, February 2021.

A carbon tax ultimately will impose burdens on the less well-off. For example, in airline travel, the planes have become much more efficient, reducing emissions per passenger mile, but the number of people flying has soared, as plane travel has become affordable to the average person.[10] In the case of fossil fuels (like gasoline), the increased taxes are likely to be regressive, imposing a greater burden on the average family than on the wealthy. The financial impact could be offset by transfer payments; but, in the end, if there is to be a reduction in the burning of fossil fuels, that reduction will have to be, at least initially, at the expense of those who would otherwise be doing the burning. At a minimum, those persons would have to do less burning. In other words, the working poor need to drive less, and any compensation cannot simply be used to maintain the levels of prior activities.

This fact poses a real problem for Democrats. As Jenkins subsequently observed: "In 2008, after the Obama Democrats won full control in Washington, Al Gore had an epiphany: Unpopular, tax-like measures were no longer necessary. The climate problem could be solved with subsidies. Who doesn't like a handout? A proposed oil tax disappeared from the Obama campaign website. Overnight, the Democratic focus went from climate policy to climate pork." Holman W. Jenkins, Jr., "Biden's Climate Is Serious—About Green Pork," WSJ.com, July 17, 2020. The Biden Administration is now in a bind. The subsidies have not reduced carbon emissions (the rather dramatic reductions in the U.S. have come largely from the increased use of natural gas—enabled by fracking). Biden needs something that appears dramatic, but does not place burdens on the working-class voters. So, no carbon tax. Instead, he acts to obstruct North American oil and gas production (the obvious "bad" guys), while simultaneously encouraging OPEC to expand production so gas prices do not go up. What a plan! Carbon emissions are unaffected, more money flows from the U.S. to the OPEC nations (including Russia), yet Green "Brownie points" are earned. A "win", except for the American people. Oh, and let's also increase subsidies.

Obviously, a carbon tax would not alleviate the global problem unless widely adopted among the nations. Some pressure might be exerted on reluctant nations through tariffs that would indirectly collect the tax, but the free-rider problem will likely persist. That fact presents a policy dilemma that may not be so easy to resolve but cannot be ignored. But, we can afford some number of free riders (as all societies do). And, as technological and cultural changes occur, other nations are likely to follow the leaders.

A carbon tax has sometimes been described as an "insurance policy", which of course it is not. I think of it as simply hedging one's bets. Hedging can often be a sensible public policy choice, to reduce risks modestly at a moderate cost, especially in the face of uncertainty.

So, in short, is it better to incentivize human ingenuity (i) to seek to reduce carbon emissions or (ii) to seek to reap government benefits? Where do we want the talent directed?

ENDNOTES

[1] In February 1861, John Tyndall gave a lecture at the Royal Society in London reporting on his recent studies of the role of heat-absorbing gases in the atmosphere on global temperatures. Peter Moore, "The Great Victorian Weather Wars," *The New York Times*, August 7, 2015.

[2] The range has been 1.5C to 4.5C in each report, except for 2007 (4AR) when it was 2.0C to 4.5C. The IPCC then went back to the prior estimat-

ed range. Lewis and Crok, "A Sensitive Matter," at 19 (Table 1). In AR6, the range is 2.5C to 4.0C. That is considerably narrower.

[3] David Rose, "And now it's global COOLING! Return of Arctic ice cap as it grows by 29% in a year," *MailOnline*, 8 September 2013 (reporting on the corrected figures from the NSIDC–National Snow and Ice Data Centre–showing that the Arctic ice cover had increased significantly from the prior year, apparently due to a cool Arctic summer in 2013 and noting that the BBC had reported on 12 December 2007 the forecasts of the disappearance of Arctic sea ice by the summer of 2013). But, the winter of 2013-14 was warmer than usual in the Arctic (while colder in the eastern United States), resulting in slower growth of the sea ice, leaving the extent of ice in February to be the fourth lowest recorded by satellite data since 1979. (February 2005 was the lowest on record). NSIDC, "In the Arctic, winter's might doesn't have much bite," *Arctic Sea Ice News & Analysis*, March 3, 2014. The sea ice in the Bering Sea was down somewhat, but had been at record levels in recent years. "On July 15, Arctic sea ice extent stood ... below the record for July 15, set in 2011. This places extent at the lowest level for this time of year on the satellite record. ... By contrast, extent north of Alaska is near the 1981 to 2010 average for this time of year." NSIDC, "Siberian downward slide," *Arctic Sea Ice News & Analysis*, July 15, 2020.

[4] "In the last decade, Antarctic sea ice has experienced both its highest and lowest extents in the satellite record [starting in the late 1970s]. The years 2012, 2013, and 2014 brought record highs; 2017 and 2018 brought record lows. Starting in 2016, Antarctica sea ice extent was mostly below the 1981–2010 average. ...Long story short: Climate change has a discernible influence on Arctic sea ice, but it has a complicated, messy influence on Antarctic sea ice." Michon Scott, "Understanding climate: Antarctic sea ice extent," NOAA *Climate.gov*, April 28, 2020.

[5] "Because the higher ECS values in some models are related to cloud feedbacks and cloud-aerosol interactions, a major research question that needs to be pursued is what is the actual nature and magnitude of cloud feedbacks in general and cloud-aerosol interactions in particular." Gerald A. Meehl, Catherine A. Senior, *et al.*, "Context for interpreting equilibrium climate sensitivity and transient climate response from the CMIP6 Earth system models," *Science Advances*, Vol. 6, no. 26, 24 June 2020.

[6] "David Nolan, a professor in the Department of Atmospheric Sciences ... said slow-moving hurricanes are not altogether unusual, ... it can be just

a matter of bad luck. Nolan said he agreed that global warming is driving increased rainfall but added that it has been harder to draw links between hurricanes and other effects of climate change. ...[I]t has been suggested that global warming could strengthen storms by making the strongest hurricanes even more intense. But so far, ... there has been no evidence that such a trend exists." Id.

[7] "The reason for the emergence of the new seep remains a mystery, but it is probably not global heating, as the Ross Sea where it was found has yet to warm significantly." Id.

[8] Indeed, the declining population growth rate is continuing:

> "For some time, demographers have been scaling back forecasts of future population growth, but they may not have gone far enough. A new University of Washington study... predicts some startling changes over the course of the century. Instead of the global population reaching between 9.4 billion and 12.7 billion by 2100 (as estimated in the 2019 United Nations World Population Prospects report), the new study suggests it will peak at 9.7 billion in 2064 and then decrease to about 8.8 billion by 2100."

Walter Russell Mead, "Snooze the Climate Alarms: A new study predicts population will drop sharply as developing economies grow," WSJ.com, July 27, 2020.

[9] Secretary of State John Kerry urged Indonesia to combat climate change, noting the potentially devastating effects it may have on that country, but he could identify no specific steps that Indonesia could take, only programs [that] would help protect its ports and infrastructure from the consequences of global warming. See Michael R. Gordon and Coral Davenport, "Kerry Implores Indonesia on Climate Change Peril," *The New York Times*, February 16, 2014. Kerry's meeting with President Susilo Bambang Yudhoyono was reportedly canceled because the President was focused on relief efforts following a deadly volcanic eruption. Id.

[10] "[N]ew research ... found that emissions from global air travel [accounting currently for only 2.5% of manmade carbon emissions] may be increasing more than 1.5 times as fast as the U.N. estimate. ... 'Airlines ... are becoming more fuel efficient. But we're seeing demand outstrip any of that,' ... ." Hiroko Tabuchi, "Worse Than Anyone Expected': Air Travel Emissions Vastly Outpace Predictions," *The New York Times*, September 20, 2019.

A Proposal for Tax Reform

There are many social and policy problems that present true dilemmas, sometimes because of deep, irreconcilable differences in values, sometimes because of a genuine lack of understanding (of the facts and/or of the relevant causal relationships) and sometimes because of both. Tax does not seem to me to be one of those subjects. Take out personal interest and any non-tax political agenda and identify the legitimate goals of tax policy, and the answers suggest themselves.

Setting the Stage

Proper goals of a tax system

We want our tax system to reflect certain objectives in addition to sufficient revenue collection. First, the system should be generally fair (an income tax should tax actual income and do so on a reasonable basis reflecting some combination of benefits received, ability to pay and consumption of society's resources). Second, the system should minimize the distortion of the allocation of resources and the incentives to engage in wasteful and nonproductive activities. Third, the system should be designed and implemented so that compliance is high (with opportunities to cheat or evade tax as limited as reasonably possible). Finally, the system should give most of the population a stake in the costs of the operation of government. An additional objective advocated by many is that the system be progressive (for the explicit purpose of redistributing income).

The first three of these objectives would probably be pretty widely accepted. Most people would likely agree that it would be better if a significant portion of our national human resources (and our individual time) were not spent in tax planning or "gaming" the tax system and that there be a high degree of compliance with the rules that are in place. The reductions of wasted resources, gaming and cheating could all be promoted by a system that is simple, with a minimum of special provisions and "loopholes". They will also be promoted by lower marginal rates, making the gaming and cheating less profitable.

A smaller, but probably still a large, number of people would agree that tax incentives that redirect investment and efforts into less productive activities are undesirable, at least in theory. Obviously, there is support for tax incentives designed to encourage socially useful activity. The problem is that, in my opinion, such social planning often has consequences other than what was intended. Moreover, programs that offer money or benefits from the government clearly encourage gaming and manipulation, as well as fraud and corruption.

The other two objectives—a broad base and a progressive structure—may be subject to more debate. I do not intend to engage in such debate here. My interest is simply in outlining the implications for tax policy if one accepts these objectives. My proposals below would result in a very progressive tax system with a broad base.

I do not consider an analysis of who benefits most or least from tax provisions to be a legitimate tax policy consideration. It certainly should not be the only or primary criterion by which a tax bill is judged, as it was for critics of the 2017 Act. If the structure is right, the burdens can be adjusted through the tax rates.

Difficulties with data

Before undertaking that analysis, however, I want to comment briefly on some issues concerning data and facts. We can discuss certain of the "rules", like the marginal tax rates for various groups or particular deductions or special rates (*e.g.*, capital gains) in the abstract; but, it can also be interesting to see what is happening in practice. For that investigation, however, we need to know what people actually pay on what they actually receive.

Such information would seem to be especially important for discussions of the consequences of different tax rates in different countries, since the relationship between the rates on the books and the amounts actually paid varies significantly from country to country. The reasons involve attitudes toward and practices concerning compliance and enforcement, as well as differences in the treatment of different geographical sources of income and the rules concerning tax residency. For example, the United States taxes its citizens on worldwide income; many other countries do not.

For many reasons, we would also want to know the amounts of income received but not captured by the system, such as the income arising in the cash or black-market economy, the unreported income of non-employees and the non-taxed "perks" provided to employees (cars, lunches, childcare, etc.).

Much of this information is simply not available. The gaps in knowledge of the facts become particularly great in efforts to compare the situations in different nations, but they are still very serious within the U.S. Thus, much of the more inflamed rhetoric about taxes can and should be dismissed simply on the basis of its reliance on unreliable data.

Revisions to the current US System

There are, of course, several proposals for the radical restructuring of our tax system. Those proposals could be analyzed using the same criteria discussed above. At this time, however, I shall be addressing our current structure and suggesting "modest" revisions that, in my opinion, would dramatically improve the functioning of the system.

Payroll and Income Taxes

I am assuming as a primary objective that everyone, within reason, should pay income tax and, thereby, have some financial "skin" in the choices among government policies and programs.

To that end, I would eliminate payroll taxes on employees. They are premised, I think most agree, on a seriously misleading characterization of Social Security as a personal savings plan, and they are simply a complication that confuses the analysis of tax burdens. The "contributions" are not deductible and the subsequent payments are fully taxed. The tax also burdens earned income specifically. Moreover, the payroll tax, including the charge for Medicare, invites avoidance. *See, e.g.*, Christy Bieber, "Biden's Tax Returns Show Why His Payroll Tax Plan May Not Save Social Security," *The Motley Fool*, September 13, 2020 ("To understand the problem with Biden's plan to raise payroll taxes, you just need to take a look at his tax returns from 2017 and 2018. They show how the Bidens were able to avoid paying hundreds of thousands of dollars in payroll taxes that fund Medicare.") These taxes are also frequently evaded in the cash ("off-the-books") economy by small businesses and individuals .

Then, I would impose a minimum 10% income tax on all income above a relatively modest personal exemption (say $10,000 per person, capped at $40,000 for a family). Further, as a matter of fairness, I would have progressive rates above the 10% minimum Personally, I think it is oppressive to be taxed more than one-third of one's income, but I recognize that we probably need higher rates to generate sufficient revenue. So, I would propose a top rate of 35%, with a special 50% rate imposed on income above $10 million a year. I justify this special rate on the debatable ground that certain income levels are just outside of the norms by which we should determine policy. Where the steps between 10% and 35% occur should be a matter of meeting legitimate revenue needs.

I would prefer, thereafter, that increases in the Federal budget that require more tax revenue be met by proportional increases in all marginal rates (say 10%, bringing the bottom rate to 11% and the top rate to 38.5%). In that way we would all share the burden of more spending.

DEDUCTIONS

Deductions are obviously controversial, because many individual interests are at stake.

As one of the many supposed beneficiaries of the 2017 Tax Act who pay significantly more income tax as a result of the Act, I understand the appeal of deductions for state and local income taxes (if such taxes are essentially based upon total adjusted gross income), on the grounds that income taxes imposed by any source reduce income and the ability to consume (unlike sales taxes or a VAT-type tax, both of which effectively tax consumption). However, to address the question rationally, one must decide which is the first or primary tax. It is the secondary income tax where the deduction for taxes paid belongs. Thus, if the state or locality taxed Federal net after-tax income only (allowing a deduction for Federal income taxes paid), then a Federal deduction would not be appropriate.

One should view a 10% state income tax on AGI as really a 16.2% tax on net income, assuming a 38% Federal rate. And, the higher the Federal rate, the higher the effective state net rate will be. Perhaps this way of looking at the issue would be useful. I think that most would view the Federal tax as primary. This approach also identifies the real burdens of state and local taxes.

There is no reason to allow an income tax deduction for local property taxes. Like the mortgage interest deduction, it is just a subsidy for home ownership.

(House Democrats seek to restore larger deductions for state and local income and property taxes, eliminating the Trump tax increase on high earners in high-tax states, like me.)

I would allow deductions for charitable contributions, but I would eliminate the benefits from contributing appreciated assets. The deduction should be limited to the basis in the asset (or the appreciation should be recognized at the time of the contribution). Not only would such a rule be fair, it would reduce controversies over valuation. But, I would phase out the mortgage deduction or, at least, limit it to principle residences (with only one per family) and impose a lower cap (say $250,000 of debt). Similarly, I would eliminate the deduction for property taxes.

Capital Gains

With respect to capital gains (and dividend income, next), I look to what I consider to be the stronger fairness arguments that have been made.

A capital asset held for a long period will generally have suffered a serious impact from inflation. Thus, the apparent gain is often largely not gain at all. The relevant test is what would the sale price realized enable the seller to buy in terms of some representative basket of goods. If the basket has not increased in size, then how can one say that the seller had income?

This consideration may not be of particular relevance with respect to certain types of capital gain, however. Someone who invests $10,000 in a startup business and ends up with stock worth $10,000,000 after a few years has clearly enjoyed significant gain. There may be policy reasons for preferential tax rates on such gain, but the inflation factor is not one of them. In contrast, the person who buys a house for $200,000 and sells it for $350,000 some 30 years later may have actually lost money on the investment.

Indexing the cost basis for inflation and taxing the resulting gain at normal ordinary income rates would be the fairest solution. It would also happen to eliminate the current issues about "carried interests" and stock options, since there would be little or no cost basis to index. (For the purist, gain should be recognized on long-term debt as reduced by inflation.)

Absent indexing, I would suggest a capital gain tax rate of half the otherwise applicable income tax rate for assets held for at least 3 years and 25% of the otherwise applicable rate for assets held for at least 10 years. Gains on sales of assets held less than 3 years should be ordinary income. Thus, much of the speculative trading would be treated as ordinary-income-generating activity. In addition, I would treat "carried interests" as ordinary income, taxed when realized. None of the fairness arguments for capital gains applies to such compensation, which is received for services rendered and is not based on a capital asset subject to inflation risk. The same approach would apply to all stock options and other incentive compensation schemes.

Dividends

The argument against taxing dividends is that the income has already been taxed once at the corporate level. The solution I propose is to provide the corporation with a deduction from current income for dividends paid during the tax year. To the recipient, the dividend would be ordinary income. If the corporation elects to hold or invest the income (or use the funds for stock buybacks), then it would be taxed on that income as a result of that decision. In such a case, the corporation would retain the benefit of the income generated. If the income is subsequently distributed as a dividend, it would be taxed again to the recipient, but I would argue that there would have been two taxable events in that case, justifying two taxes.

Business Taxes

Publicly-traded corporations should be taxed at a low rate (say 20%), with a deduction for dividends paid, as discussed above.

These corporations should also be taxed on the same accounting basis that they use to report results. I suggest that their fiscal year should also be their tax year. Eliminating the two sets of books would result in cost savings, the incentives for managers would be better aligned (currently, there are strong incentives to have low income for tax purposes and high income for stock market purposes) and resources devoted to tax "planning" would be reduced.

> *"Corporations are required to report income to investors according to generally accepted accounting principles, which are set by the private standards-setting Financial Accounting Standards*

> Board (FASB). But Congress writes the tax code. Most differences between financial and taxable income were created by Congress to encourage certain business spending. These include tax credits for research and development, green energy and low-income housing. ..[Also,] accelerated depreciation, which lets companies immediately expense investment in equipment. This contrasts with financial accounting, which requires companies to depreciate assets roughly tracking their decline in productivity."

The Editorial Board, "Kyrsten Sinema Reads the Book Tax," WSJ.com, August 4, 2022.

For all privately-held corporations or limited-liability entities (as well as all unincorporated businesses), I would tax the owners on the income as if they were in a partnership, with no tax on the entity itself. Thus, the earnings would all be taxed at the individual earned income rates applied to the percentage ownerships. To the extent that earnings are retained in the entity, the cost bases of the owners would be increased. The deduction for pass-through entities (currently 20%) should be eliminated. It has no justification. Under this approach, I think that certain abuses could be more clearly isolated and discouraged (including the payroll tax issue mentioned above).

Finally, much stricter rules should be imposed concerning the allocation of income among countries of operation. I would simply require that for multinational corporate groups (companies with, say, more than 50% common ultimate ownership) operating in the United States (regardless of domicile), the income allocated to the US be no less as a percentage of total income than the revenues derived in the US represents as a percentage of total revenues of the group. Thus, the repatriation of earnings from abroad to the United States would not be a taxable event. Also, the choice of location for the "headquarters" or the incorporation of the entity would not be influenced by US income tax.

ESTATE TAXES

My preference, based on reasons like those set forth concerning the income tax, would be either to eliminate the estate tax or to have an exemption of $20 million, with a rate applied to the next $30 million of 25% and a rate of 40% for amounts above $50 million. If the amount of the exemption were to be raised and the rate lowered as suggested, I would eliminate the marital deduction.

For appreciated assets subject to the estate tax (40%), a stepped-up basis for the beneficiaries makes sense. It is excessive to tax the gain again when the asset is sold. However, elimination of the stepped-up basis would reduce some of the perceived need for the estate tax. So, I suggest that for estates not subject to the estate tax, appreciated assets, like individually-owned businesses (including farms) and family homes, be included in the estate at their cost bases (not at their fair market value). The gain would be taxed (at applicable capital gains rates, based upon combined ownership periods) only when the asset is sold and the gain realized by the beneficiaries. (Note, this approach is very different from President Biden's current proposal.)

Various Other Matters

I would liberalize the rules concerning retirement plans. As long as there are requirements restricting the access to the funds or penalizing early withdrawals, I would continue to allow the gains to accrue tax-free. The limits on the annual contributions should be raised (say to $500,000), with only a much lower amount to be deductible (say $10,000). When distributions are allowed, they should be treated as return of capital (for the after-tax contributions) and as ordinary income (for the gain and the deductible portions). I also favor more regulations to discourage the cash or black market economy. To some extent, at the same time, lower, fairer tax rates would promote compliance and make avoidance and evasion less appealing.

I would also favor a straight 10% tax on all currently tax-exempt income and eliminate the Alternative Minimum Tax completely.

Lastly, I would support the elimination of all tax subsidies and incentives. (I have no issue with the taxing of undesirable activities or of activities with externalities that the market cannot capture, but such taxes should not be characterized as income taxes.) If it is decided that an activity should be subsidized, it should be done so directly rather than through the income tax system. The allocative distortions will be less, the cost more clearly revealed and the decision to subsidize more transparent.

A Note Reflecting the Current Politic Climate

There is now near hysteria among parts of the media and various politicians over income and wealth inequality, which has led to a focus on taxes. The rich do not pay their "fair share."

Tax avoidance

In 2021, *ProPublica* combed through a "trove" of illegally disclosed IRS information about wealthy Americans to expose how the rich "avoid" paying taxes. The result makes no claim of finding tax evasion, nor even shady tax avoidance. Instead, it "discovers," for example, that of the rare entrepreneurs (out of millions) who are extraordinarily successful, a handful choose not to "cash in" but maintain ownership of the companies they founded and built. Not surprisingly, these individuals now are many of the ultra-wealthy. Also, not surprisingly, those few paid little income tax relative to their enormous wealth.

Of course, had these individuals sold much of their interests early, they would be much less wealthy today and would have paid much more in tax. And, other people would be wealthier today if they had sold their investments and paid tax, rather than holding on while the values dropped.

As for the policy implications, would we all really be better off if the successful individuals had "cashed out"? If these ultra-wealthy continue to hold these assets until death, a 40% estate tax will be due on the fair market value, unless they utilize the "loophole" of giving the assets to charity (which many ultra-wealthy today are pledging to do). Would we all really be better off if that money goes to the government instead?

All that was news for me was the assertion that in the 1920s, the Congressional decision not to tax as income unrealized capital gains was highly controversial because it created a major "loophole": Build a successful company, borrow against it, then die, leaving it to charity. Wow. You might wonder why not everyone does it.

ProPublica also "found" a technique to avoid tax that does not require dying. Before you are wealthy, create a Roth IRA, buy some very, very cheap assets that will subsequently soar in value, watch your investment grow tax free, then withdraw the money tax free after you turn 59 1/2. We should all have done this.

These examples reflect totally legal behavior. The fact that tax was (legally) avoided is almost coincidental. These remarkable situations did not arise through astute tax planning. They arose because a few people were extraordinarily lucky or extraordinarily astute or both. Of course, the rules can be changed, but one should not base tax policy on the flukes or exceptional cases.

Tax "evasion"

The media in mid-2021 has also been full of stories proclaiming that the rich evade taxes more than others. The assertion is based on a working paper published earlier in the year: John Guyton, Patrick Langetieg, Daniel Reck, Max Risch, Gabriel Zucman, "Tax Evasion at the Top of the Income Distribution: Theory and Evidence," *equitablegrowth.org*, March 2021. That paper hardly establishes the proposition.

The authors conclude that two methods of evasion most difficult for auditors to find are off-shore bank accounts (significantly reduced today by new reporting requirements) and abuse of pass-through business entities, which the authors say are most used by the rich. The support is that the reported income by pass-through entities is heavily weighted in favor of those with the highest reported income. What we are interested in, instead, is the unreported income. Small business owners use pass-through entities, and they are numerous. Do they underreport income? Of course.

There are also other sources of unreported income that are difficult to detect on audit, like the "cash economy " and illegal activities (crime). These sources logically are more likely to be enjoyed by the less rich in terms of reported income. The "cash economy" is estimated at 10-13% of GDP. Criminal proceeds, including fraud, is probably as much. So, 20-26% of additional GDP. The top quintile in reported income represents about 60% of the total. Assuming the other 4 quintiles report 40% of the income **and** these types of unreported income goes mainly to them, the actual income of the 4 lower quintiles goes up by some 40-50%.

The authors correctly observe that the current income categories are based on reported income only. The members of each category would change if unreported income were included. That is, the identities of many of the "rich" would be different. Indeed, the failure to report income is probably much more common among those who are not rich by reported income than among those who are. The authors seem to realize that, but do not explore what it means.

So, in short, the media consensus view of tax evasion by those who the media thinks are the rich is false.

In September 2021, the Treasury Department stated: "Today, the "tax gap"—the difference between taxes that are owed and collected—totals around $600 annually... . The tax gap can be a major source of inequity. ... [E]stimates from academic researchers [just discussed] suggest that more than $160 billion lost annually is from taxes that top 1 percent choose not to pay." Natasha Sarin, "The Case for a Robust Attack on the Tax Gap," September 7, 2021. The Commissioner of the IRS recently testified before Congress that the tax gap may be as high as $1 trillion.

So, the top 1% may account for 16% to 27% of the total tax gap. But, the top 1% receives over 20% of the reported income and pays 40% of the total income taxes. Thus, the alleged $160 billion is neither "excessive" nor "unequal" on its face! The claims about tax evasion increasing inequality are simply unsupported. Moreover, much more could be gained by closing the gap for the 99%.

Ironically, the Treasury proclaims: "The Administration has been clear that audit rates will not rise relative to recent years for those with under $400,000 in actual income." *Id.* But, absent the audits, the IRS will not know the actual incomes, only the reported. The message is clear: a straight forward invitation to evade tax!

We can agree that among those with similar actual incomes, those who do not report much of it will be richer than those who do report. We may conclude that the "rich" evade more taxes than the non-rich; but the rich are just not who we think they are. And, so-called "tax cuts for the rich" are really tax cuts for those who pay taxes. You cannot cut taxes for those who pay none already.

"FAIR SHARE"

Now for "fair shares". The top 1% pays 40% of total collected individual income taxes, the top 20% pays 80%, the bottom 40-60% pays effectively 0%. Are those shares fair? Is it "fair" for more than 40% of the population to pay nothing for the protections and services of the Federal government? (It is certainly not good for representative government.) The top 1% receives over 20% (and the top 20% receives some 60%) of the reported income. Does that tell you what is "fair"?

What might be informative would be the percentages of income paid in taxes by the big-time lawyers making $3-5 million a year, the CEOs making $10-20 million and the fund managers making $50-100 million. Or, other members of the 1%, excluding the top 0.01%. The answer is probably between 30% and 40% of total income. That might make for a more relevant comparison with the average worker.

What is clearly not fair is the amount of taxes paid by those who do not report their income. On that, most of us can agree. So, we should try to reduce tax evasion. But, increased marginal tax rates will not help that problem. It would probably aggravate it. And, more audits focused on the persons with high reported income, as is being advocated, is not the answer. The important types of evasion, we have discussed, are not easily found through audits. Moreover, persons with high reported income are probably not the serious tax evaders.

Concluding Comments

The main benefits that I see from my proposals are:

- the favorable realignment of incentives affecting behavior and the allocation of society's resources;
- increased simplicity, reducing compliance costs and uncertainty;
- more compliance, because of clarity and lower costs;
- greater fairness and
- the presentation to voters of a more rational choice as to the impact of increased government spending—it will be harder to push the costs on to others, and increased spending would have an impact on a greater percentage of the electorate.

Of course, the current Biden plan is quite different in detail and philosophy. Its focus is primarily on who pays, presuming that 'fairness" is only a matter of relative tax burden—with the more skewed or progressive, the "fairer," with certain exceptions for Democratic strongholds. This proposed plan achieves none of the objectives with which I started, not even the generation of sufficient revenue. It offers none of the benefits of my proposals. As a matter public policy, it is myopic—a monument to political expediency.

"AntiReligion" and Sam Harris

The proponents

> "At the dawn of the new atheist movement [2007], the thinkers who became known as 'the four horsemen', the heralds of religion's unraveling—Christopher Hitchens, Richard Dawkins, Sam Harris, and Daniel Dennett—sat down together over cocktails. What followed was a rigorous, pathbreaking, and enthralling exchange that has been viewed millions of times since it was first posted on YouTube."

Amazon.com, *Audible*, 2019.

Somewhat curiously, we have seen over the past 20 years the appearance of a vocal group of philosopher-scientists purportedly committed to the elimination of traditional religion, persons like Sam Harris, Daniel Dennett and Richard Dawkins. See, *e.g.*, Rupert Sheldrake, *The Science Delusion: Freeing the Spirit of Inquiry* (2012), pp.24-5. They seem to occupy a niche specialty, sometimes referred to as "the public understanding of science". Harris, educated in philosophy and neuroscience, is CEO of Project Reason, a nonprofit organization supposedly focused on spreading scientific knowledge and secular values. Richard Dawkins, whose academic training was in zoology, was the Charles Sionyi Professor of the Public Understanding of Science at Oxford University. Is there a scientific discipline consisting of the criticism of religion? (By the way, Christopher Hitchens, *e.g.*, *God Is Not Great: How Religion Poisons Everything* (2007), was an essayist and social critic, not a scientist or philosopher, like the other three.)

The defensiveness of their attacks may seem hard to comprehend, given the apparent acceptance of Darwinism in the educated community as a whole. In addition, their efforts also seem inconsistent with their underlying assumption of a lack of free will, since these advocates speak and write as if the audience is capable of changing its mind. The image of modern science based upon the model of physics is essentially materialistic and deterministic, rather than organic and purposeful. Such were the philosophical assumptions on which much of modern science was constructed. When applied to the human mind, the necessary conclusion from such science is that we lack free will. That is not an inference from physical or empirical evidence, but a logical conclusion from the assumptions on which the science was based. See Sheldrake, *The Science Delusion*, pp.9, 17. The conclusion, of course, sharply conflicts with most religious beliefs.

The purported clash between science and religion, about which I have written elsewhere, has apparently captured the interest of a sizable portion of the reading public. For example, the billing for a book by John Paul Paulos entitled *Antireligion* (2009) proclaims: "A mathematician explains why the arguments for God just don't add up." The author is a well respected mathematician and has written several books of popularized mathematics. My complaint is not about the content or positions advanced—he discusses and attempts to disprove several logical arguments for the existence of God that have appeared over the ages and does so with insight and clarity—but with the title and the implication that his credentials as a mathematician make him particularly well-suited to the task or give his arguments some special weight. In fact, the arguments—pro and con—are readily accessible to the lay reader. There is nothing about his academic credentials that entitle his views on the subject to be given any special deference. Perhaps the offending language and implications are primarily attributable to the publisher or publicist engaged to promote sales of the book, but the fact that they believe that such an angle would be productive supports my belief that there is something unfortunate going on.

Of course, there are scientists who speak out in support of religion. Dr. Hugh Ross, a published astrophysicist, regularly writes and speaks as an advocate of Christian faith and doctrine. *See, e.g., Time and Creation* (1994). His scientific credentials are prominently cited; however, he uses his knowledge of science to make and support his arguments, not just as credentials to give extra weight to his advocacy of unrelated positions. Another such scientist is Francis S. Collins, the former head of the public Human Genome Project in the United States. *See, e.g., The Language of God* (2006). Similarly, recently deceased physicist Ian Barbour was an outspoken advocate for the coexistence of and regular dialogue between science and religion, inspiring other scientists to seek to reconcile the two. William Yardley, "Ian Barbour, Who Found a Balance Between Faith and Science, Dies at 90," *The New York Times*, January 12, 2014. One can also look at the writings of physicist Paul Davies, *e.g., The Mind of God: The Sci-*

entific Basis for a Rational World (1992), and evolutionary biologist/paleontologist Simon Conway Morris, *e.g.*, *The Crucible of Creation* (1998); *Life's Solution: Inevitable Humans in a Lonely Universe* (2003).

Richard Dawkins, in his 2006 best seller, made many statements that are similar to the early assertions of Sam Harris, but presented them not as factual or logical arguments but as supposedly self-evident propositions. *The God Delusion*, pp.23–4. (Dawkins' principle argument there and elsewhere is that neo-Darwinism based upon natural selection has been so decisively established as the scientific explanation for life on Earth that the religious doctrines of the past are not only no longer needed but can now be seen to be delusions arising out of ignorance. *Id.*, pp.32–3, 85, 137–89. I discuss this argument elsewhere.) Since I have already written about the unnecessary and destructive conflicts between science and religion, I focus here on the evolving positions of Sam Harris.

VIOLENCE AND RELIGION

Sam Harris became quite a successful (*i.e.*, bestselling) author by engaging in vehement attacks on religion in the form of purported historical and logical arguments. *See, e.g.*, *The End of Faith: Religion, Terror, and the Future of Reason* (2005). In brief, his thesis is that religion has been the cause of much of the brutality and savagery in human history and has been so to such an extent that the discrediting and elimination of organized religion would make the world a less violent and more humane place. His supporting evidence is the ample history of violence and butchery that has occurred in the name of religion. *See, e.g.*, id., p.26. His thesis is provocative; it turns upside down the more traditional form of the question: how religion has so often been co-opted by the forces of evil, to which religion should be opposed, in order to do evil.

That evidence is vast and truly depressing. But, as support for Harris' thesis, it is wholly inadequate.

First, it is obvious that not all or even most violent acts can be connected to religion. Start with the individual acts regularly reported by our news media and that are addressed by our criminal courts. Next, broaden the examination of the historical episodes of genocide, exploitation and repression. Does religion explain the Congo or Rwanda or Vietnam or Cambodia? Or, Stalin's 20 million?[*] Or China's Cultural Revolution? Does it even explain the events in Nazi Germany? (Harris asserts: "Knowingly or not, the Nazis were agents of religion." *The End of Faith*, p.79. Knowingly or not? His reasoning is discussed in the next paragraphs.) While not irrelevant, perhaps, religion also does not seem to have been the cause of the extermination of indigenous populations in the Americas and certainly not of the North Atlantic slave trade.

Second, even where religion was clearly implicated in the events, what is Mr. Harris' basis for asserting that the religious fervor or commitment was the cause of the violence, rather than merely an available excuse or justification? In other words, why would we think that the violence would not have occurred if religion had not existed? Clearly, it has been possible for religion to have been used to rally, organize and motivate group violence; but, the causes of that violence could well lay somewhere else in the human psyche or in cultural institutions or in forms of economic organization.

According to Harris, our beliefs are "leading us, inexorably, to kill one another." *Id.*, p.12. The argument is: "As a man believes, so will he act." *Id.*, p.44. Even if that were more or less true, how do we know what persons actually believe? Harris relies on surveys, like Gallup polls, in which people were asked about their religious beliefs. *See id.*, p.17. He also examines various religious texts and extracts the portions that exhort the use of violence. (With respect to Islam, he purports to assess the relative frequency of excerpts that urge violence compared to those that urge tolerance and finds the former greatly predominant.) He then claims that men like Osama bin Laden "actually believe what they say they believe" (*id.*, p.29) and finds it surprising that, given the beliefs that he finds evidenced by the texts, the violence is not even more pervasive (*id.*, p.33).

I do not find that fact so surprising. I would say that despite the responses to surveys and the content of the Koran and of various parts of the Bible, what people really believe is much more nuanced than Harris asserts and that what will motivate people to action is much more complex than what they believe. I do not doubt, however, that what people say they believe can contribute to their response to the exigencies of particular situations, like crowd pressure, or can provide justifications for actions that they desire to undertake for other reasons.

Harris' thesis concerning the cause of violence is directly addressed by Karen Armstrong in her book *Fields of Blood: Religion and the History of Violence* (2014).

Armstrong finds violence to be a likely, perhaps inevitable, outcome of the transition from the prehistoric, hunter-gatherer *Homo sapiens* to modern man. Agriculture leads to large communities; large communities require coercion to maintain order and allocate output (and surplus production); coercion leads to an elite that flourishes on (and then requires) the surplus production of the masses; the elite enables the development of culture and civilization—the arts, the sciences, technology, and so on. Armstrong's approach anchors violence in the evolution of mankind, both biological and societal, referring to "the violence embedded in our human nature and the nature of the state, which from the start required forcible subjugation of at least 90% of the population." *Id.*, p.394. Armstrong also makes the point that the identification of religion as something separate from society and politics did not even occur until the seventeenth and eighteen centuries. *Id.*

However, this explanation may also be over-simplistic. Recent archeological discoveries indicate a much more varied and complicated history. *See* David Graeber and David Wengrow, *The Dawn of Everything: A New History of Humanity* (2021). For example, "over tens of thousands of years, we see monuments and magnificent burials, but little else to indicate the growth of ranked societies, let alone anything remotely resembling 'states'." *Id.*, p.92. There is "further evidence that Bronze Age cities—the world's first large-scale, planned human settlements—could emerge in the absence of ruling classes and managerial elites... ." *Id.*, p.313. And, "[I]t is difficult ... to make any sort of convincing argument that warfare was a significant feature of early farming societies in the Middle East, as by now one would expect some evidence for it to have shown up in the record." *Id.*, p.249. "In short, there is simply no reason to assume that the adoption of agriculture in more remote periods also meant the inception of private land ownership, territoriality, or an irreversible departure from forager egalitarianism." *Id.*, p.251. Cities and farming do not necessarily bring violence and warfare.

Similarly, a recent archeological discovery west of Lake Turkana in Kenya suggests that warfare may have appeared as early as 10,000 years ago, pre-dating agriculture there. Researchers found the remains of some 28 individuals who appear to have died from grievous violently-inflicted wounds. M. Mirazón Lahr, *et al.*, "Inter-group violence among early Holocene hunter-gatherers of West Turkana, Kenya," *Nature*, 529, 394–398, 21 January 2016. *See also*, University of Cambridge, "Earliest evidence of human warfare," *Research Bulletin*, 22 January 2016. So, warfare may also precede cities and farming.

IRRATIONALITY AND RELIGION

Harris argues that beliefs lead to actions and that religious beliefs, being irrational, lead to irrational actions. He says that acts like those of the suicide bomber are "completely unintelligible" in the absence of a belief in martyrdom and jihad or in a paradise following life on this earth. Id., p.33.

He does acknowledge in a footnote that the example of the "Tamil Tigers" of Sri Lanka appear to be a counter-example, since they are secular suicide bombers; but, he asserts, while "not explicitly religious," they "believe many improbable things about the nature of life and death" and "look on death with less alarm than seems strictly rational." Id., p.239 (n2 to page 12). (Armstrong notes that it was only after the 2004 U.S. assault on Fallujah in Iraq that the suicide bombings by Islamic terrorists from the region broke "the long-standing record of the Tamil Tigers." *Fields of Blood*, p.390.) This last comment brings us closer to Harris' real central argument, which is that since acts of terrorism and extreme violence, especially those that involve the anticipated death of the perpetrator, are irrational; they must be caused by beliefs that are irrational, of which the primary examples are religious beliefs.

The problems with this line of reasoning are quite fundamental. First, there are many sources of irrationality other than religious beliefs. Political beliefs can lead to irrational actions; as can hysteria; as can, even, poor or weak thinking or the manipulative influences of others. People are not uniformly or consistently rational. Second, many of the historical atrocities he references cannot reasonably be categorized as irrational—immoral, certainly; misguided, likely; but irrational (not reasonably calculated to achieve some desired result), no. Presumably, Harris views martyrdom even in support of peaceful causes (like the self-immolation of Tibetan Buddhist monks) as irrational and, therefore, wrong. So, irrationality seems inadequate as the basis for categorizing such actions.

But then, how do we define or identify rationality?

Take his ultimate example of irrationality—the willingness to die for a belief. Is the prevailing Western view (fear) of death rational? Is it so clearly rational to cling to the mere continuation of life regardless of its quality? Is it irrational to conclude that there are some beliefs (or values or ideas or other people) for which one would be willing to die? For that matter, why is the Western view that places such high value on individual lives rational?

A RETREAT

Harris performs a significant retreat in his 2005 Afterword, responding to comments he received on the book originally published in 2004. There he acknowledges that his criticism is not of religion as such, but of dogma and irrationality, which he says is "common" (but, obviously, not exclusive) to religion. *Id.*, p.231. Fine, but then the text of the book and most of the publicity for it are all quite misleading. And, the mischaracterizations gave rise to large sales and his public renown.

Curiously, Harris then argues that mysticism, forms of which he advocated in the book, is rational, while religion is not. *Id.*, p.226. (In the last part of his book, Harris addresses human consciousness and the still unknown world that it inhabits.) Although, Harris seemed to consider religion nonscientific because it commits to propositions that are fundamentally untestable (propositions for which there is no conceivable evidence that could constitute confirmation or refutation); in his subsequent book, *Waking Up: A Guide to Spirituality Without Religion* (2014), Harris explicitly embraces a type of spiritualism. He argues that consciousness and spiritual experiences are different from other phenomena that science studies only in that they are by definition individual–they belong to the individual experiencing them and are not readily subject to external access or verification. But, he says, they are not beyond the reach of scrutiny or disciplined analysis, so they are not beyond science.

THE MUDDLE OF THE MIDDLE

So, Harris struggles to find a middle ground between traditional religion and atheistic materialism.

He now argues that religions should not be lumped together. He strongly objects to those belief systems (like Christianity and other religions in the Abrahamic tradition) that presume dualism or a distinction between body and soul. *See, e.g., Waking Up*, pp.89-92. (He similarly objects to any approach that treats the mind as separate from or independent of the brain. He considers any such approach as non-scientific or irrational.) In contrast, Harris concludes that "Buddhism can be an entirely rational enterprise." *Id.*, p.29.

The distinction he makes is that one can allow a broad range of types of subjective experiences that can be meaningful and important while not believing that any such experiences have any relevance to the physical world. For example, "[i]t is possible to lose one's sense of being a separate self and top experience a kind of boundless, open awareness—to feel, in other words, at one with the cosmos. This says a lot about the possibilities of human consciousness, but it says nothing about the universe at large. And it sheds no light at all on the relationship between mind and matter." Id., pp.43-4.

Obviously, Harris does not believe in miracles in the form of God intervening in human affairs, but he does allow that certain paranormal phenomena like telepathy could be real. However, he notes that the lack of conclusive demonstrations of such skills in a laboratory setting suggests that such powers do not actually exist. Id., p.170. One might welcome the fact that Harris moved away from his earlier extreme and inflammatory positions, which gained him such notoriety and success, but his potentially more middle-of-the-road position is nothing but a muddle. See Gary Gutting, "Sam Harris's Vanishing Self," *The New York Times*, September 7, 2014.

Harris apparently came to appreciate some of the fallacies of his earlier stance, but has still not found the answer.

ENDNOTE

* See, e.g., Martin Amis, *Korba the Dread: Laughter and the Twenty Million* (2005) (original edition published in 2002) (setting out moving descriptions of the atrocities committed by Stalin leading to the deaths of reportedly 20 million people and criticizing the apparently unquestioning support by English liberals, including his father Kingsley, for the Soviet Union and communism); Robert Conquest, *The Great Terror: A Reassessment* (1990) (original version published in 1968). See also, Brenda Cronin and Alan Cullison, "Historian Exposed Stalin's Reign of Terror," *The Wall Street Journal*, August 5, 2015 (an obituary for Robert Conquest, noting that subsequent disclosed showed that his assessment of Stalin's reign was much closer to the actual facts than that of many of his critics).

On Nationalism

Three new books address the recent apparent rise in nationalism around the world: *The Virtue of Nationalism* (2018), by Yoram Hazony; *The Nationalist Revival* (2018), by John B. Judis; and *Identity* (2018), by Francis Fukuyama. Hazony's book is primarily political theory, with incidental references to current events. In contrast, Judis largely just describes what is currently happening in various countries. Fukuyama presents a combination of theory and description.

Nationalism and Identity

All three authors agree that nationalism traditionally depends upon the existence of a common language, a common religion and very similar customs and traditions. It is also typically associated with a specific geographical area. Often, there was or had been a common adversary or enemy. In general, the members of a nation would have a common ethnicity, but Fukuyama considers a common religion to be the most crucial element in the emergence of nations. Fukuyama, *The Origins of Political Order* (2011), pp. 59-63.

It seems to me that some form of racism is a natural and inevitable stage in the evolution of the nation-state, the result of defining one's community in contrast to others. Indeed, it may also be a necessary part of mankind's evolution as a social animal. But, it need not be the final stage. For example, Fukuyama presents the United States as a successful example of a "creedal" nation, a nation based upon a commitment to a recognized creed, reflected in a set of foundational documents and principles. The idea is that people of different ethnicities, religions, family traditions and, perhaps, even languages can bond together to form a successful nation based upon common commitment to shared civic and political values. Certainly, in America today, ethnicity is not a defining factor of membership. Nor is religion.

The strength of the nation as a unit of political order is that membership would typically be perceived as a matter of identity, shared interests and shared destiny. This is especially true for the liberal democratic nations and for other nations with a reasonable degree of individual rights and freedom. In such cases, membership can almost be viewed as consensual, as if arising from a social contract. Of course, members to do not "choose" to join, but are born into the nation. (Of course, their parents or grandparents may actually have chosen to join.) However, it is assumed that the perception of the members is that their participation is not coerced, even though there is necessarily some sacrifice of individual choice and freedom. The benefits of participation are believed easily to exceed the costs. The entire concept seems to depend upon a recognition of the nation of which they are citizens as being worthy of their loyalties and sacrifices.

This perception is especially important for liberal democratic nations and other nations with a reasonable degree of individual rights and freedom. Yet, it is assumed that the perception of the members is that their participation is not coerced but freely given. Even though there is necessarily some sacrifice of individual choice and freedom, the benefits of participation are believed easily to exceed the costs.

Over 100 years ago, in the early twentieth century, Teddy Roosevelt made a statement about immigration that would cause public outrage today:

> "[W]e should insist that if the immigrant who comes here in good faith becomes an American and assimilates himself to us, he shall be treated on an exact equality with everyone else, for it is an outrage to discriminate against any such man because of creed, or birthplace, or origin. But this is predicated upon the **person's becoming in every facet an American, and nothing but an American**... We have room for but one flag, the American flag... We have room for but one language here, and that is the English language... and we have room for but one sole loyalty and that is a loyalty to the American people."

This position is contrary to the position accepted as "politically correct" since the 1970s, but I think that it actually reflects the view of most of our good citizens today. And, it is not racism. Why should we not expect Americans to speak English? To respect our political values and institutions? Such conduct does not require the renunciation of one's own cultural heritage.

In addition, the significance of membership as part of one's identity and as a source of meaning to one's life should not be underestimated. As recently stated by New York Times columnist David Brooks:

> "Love for nation is an expanding love because it is love for the whole people. It's an ennobling love because it comes with the urge to hospitality – to share what you love and to want to make more love by extending it to others. ... If you stop the love songs to America, take the celebration of America out of public life, you leave people spiritually bereft, robbed of a great devotion."

"Yes, I'm an American Nationalist," NYTimes.com, October 25, 2018.

NATIONALISM AND SOCIAL ORDER

All three of the authors cited above agree that nationalism as a basis of political order, compared to globalism or empire, has the typical benefits that one would expect from decentralization of authority: the promotion of diversity, creativity and innovation and the prospect of positive evolution arising from competition (among various nations). (These are the benefits thought to arise from the Federal system with states' rights in the United States.) They agree that such a system of organization also tends to promote greater individual autonomy and freedom or, at least, the perception of such among the members (because they would not perceive the necessary coercion by the collective as being imposed on them by strangers or foreigners). The three authors also observed that a liberal political order based on nationalism makes possible social welfare programs, because of the belief of most that there is a common shared interest in the well-being of all members of the nation.

Such benefits are the result of the perception of legitimacy. The basis of legitimacy is the perception of consent:

> "Democracy functions on the basis of consent by the governed. Or, more accurately, it rests on the consent of the minority to be governed by the majority. Labour voters in regions that always return Conservative members of Parliament don't challenge the legitimacy of those who govern them—because they respect the political integrity of the U.K. as a whole."

Gerard Baker, "The Great Brexit Breakdown," WSJ.com, Dec. 7, 2018.

In short, national identification promotes good citizenship. But, there is more. "An important virtue of the nation-state is that it is a constraint. The contemporary peaceable nation takes what it is given—its borders and territory and resources, its citizens and tribes, its affinities and antagonisms, its history and traditions and ways of getting along—and makes the most of them." Christopher DeMuth, "America's Nationalist Awakening," *WSJ.com*, July 20, 2019. The strength of nationalism is in being a product of history:

> *"Nations evolved organically over centuries of struggle, trial and error and acquired staying power. Man is naturally social and fraternal, and successful nations have learned how to transmute group loyalties into broader allegiance. Citizens understand that their security and freedoms depend on their nation and its imperfect institutions—that their fortunes are linked for better or worse to those of their disparate compatriots."*

DeMuth, "Why America Needs National Conservatism," *WSJ.com*, November 12, 2021.

The nation-state faces its problem within the confines of its history and its established institutions. Globalism's approaches to the world's problems lack such context and grounding. The freedom from constraints and the perception of limitless options are not, in the end, good things for policy-making. Policy decisions should be made within a context and with a full recognition of the relevant history, traditions and culture.

The fact is that "[t]he nation-state remains, despite 70 years of global integration, the political unit that commands the greatest legitimacy among people. It isn't just Britain. The potential tragedy of the EU is that the continuing urge to integrate is not only ignoring this legitimacy; it is stoking the problem by further alienating voters." DeMuth, "America's Nationalist Awakening," *WSJ.com*, July 20, 2019.

Nationalism, Imperialism and Globalism

The "creedal" nation is historically highly unusual. Most multi-cultural political orders have been empires, based upon overt coercion. Hazony asserts that nationalism is concerned with matters (more or less) within the national borders (there may be disputes about the exact location of such borders), whereas globalism is by definition empire-building or imperialism, that is, focused on extending and imposing its influence and reach to other groups or nations. *The Virtue of Nationalism* (2018). Thus, Hazony adds an additional element to the definitions both of nationalism and globalism.

Leaving aside for the moment the matter of definitions, I think it is useful to distinguish between a government and people concerned with their own affairs and a government and people intent on expanding their control over others and creating an empire. If nationalism is characterized by the former, then it would be improper, for example, to call Nazi Germany or Imperial Japan examples of nationalism. (Judis does not agree, because he uses a different definition of "nationalism".) The contemporary political movements in Hungary and Poland, however, would seem to qualify as nationalism under Hazony's definition, as would Brazil (with the recent election) and, until 2022, arguably, Russia. But, not Putin's Russia now and not Xi Jinping's China:

> *"...America is preserving more than its role in the international system. It is trying to preserve the system itself—which Mr. Xi is working to overthrow by promoting imperial-era Chinese concepts. The idea that underpinned the imperial tributary system was that states near and far were obligated to acknowledge Chinese rule. Chinese emperors claimed they had the Mandate of Heaven over tianxia, or 'All Under Heaven.'"*

Gordon G. Chang, "Xi Changed My Mind About Trump: The president defends not only U.S. sovereignty but the entire world order," WSJ.com, July 24, 2019.

Hazony's dichotomy seems useful, but his unequivocal characterizations of nationalism and globalism do not, to me. He deems any political organization broader than the nation to be necessarily imperialist. For example, he is unstinting in his criticism of the European Union. The interesting question to me is whether and under what circumstances entities that would be considered nations can voluntarily join together to form a union that has the characteristics of a nation state, that is, a broad perception of common interest, of common civic values and of the relative lack of coercion. Hazony asserts that such a union is impossible.

The difficulties of the European Union are well known. Fukuyama attempts to address this question. As to the EU, he concludes that a successful union is not impossible, only not (yet) achieved. (He blames the failure on improper or inadequate implementation, and suggests various possible "fixes", such as a strengthening of the European Parliament and a curtailment of the powers of the European Commission, as well as advertising. Pretty weak stuff for such a serious challenge.) But, the challenge for the EU is more profound than Fukuyama acknowledges:

> "The 19th-century French philosopher Ernest Renan argued that 'a nation is a soul, a spiritual principle': 'These are the essential conditions of being a people: having common glories in the past and a will to continue them in the present; having made great things together and wishing to make them again. One loves in proportion to the sacrifices that one has committed and the troubles that one has suffered.'"

David Brooks, NYTimes.com, October 25, 2018.

But, how do we achieve "soul" at a multi-national or a global level if "soul" requires a history of shared sacrifice, service and commitment?

Realistically, in all events, Hazony's image of a world organized around traditional nation states is not an adequate prescription for today or the future. Cosmopolitism is a fact for the educated and well-off people around the world. Multi-culturalism is only going to increase. But, imperialism is not acceptable. So, we ask how we can retain the benefits of nationalism in a world of increasing globalization. More specifically, can a multi-national and multi-cultural form of political and community organization command from its citizens sufficient loyalty and the willingness to make sacrifices. Could the proper spirit be generated by new leaders with charisma and a vision of a reformed and broadened community? And, can such an organization stop the empire-builders?

Good Citizens and Moral Leadership

In the very early days of this country, George Washington wrote:[1]

> "the Government of the United States gives to bigotry no sanction, to persecution no assistance, requires only that they who live under its protection should demean themselves as good citizens, in giving it on all occasions their effectual support."

The emphasis was upon commitment to a type of government and civil order, backed with a willingness to provide "effectual support" as required, that is, to make sacrifices for the good of the country—to be "good citizens". It is obviously beneficial in a political order to have the vast majority of the members be "good citizens". But, what is a good citizen and what circumstances lead to the sufficient presence of them? Those are the questions addressed below.

"Good Citizens"

I grew up in southern Michigan. My parents and, as far as I could tell, most of their friends were the epitome of "good citizens". They willingly paid their taxes, were generous and supportive neighbors, participated in community activities, voted, engaged in various public displays of patriotism and made meaningful sacrifices for the country. During World War II, my father served in the US Army in Italy, while his father was a Seabee in the South Pacific.

When I moved to New York City, I was surprised to find myself surrounded by people who regularly "gamed" the system, aggressively avoiding and sometimes evading taxes, finding ways to circumvent the rules and regulations (like rent control, sales tax and parking restrictions) and, in general, constantly seeking to promote their own interests at the expense of the community (although, not necessarily at the expense of identifiable individuals).

Over 40 years ago, when I was at the University of Cambridge, I was told by some Nigerian friends that the appointment as the head of the port of Lagos was worth $1 billion. That was a lot of money back in 1970s. While, as a naïve American, I was shocked at that assertion, I was more surprised that these young aristocrats viewed the rumored fact not as a scandal, but as evidence of the opportunities for them for the future. (I was also shocked to hear my Greek friends talk about the CIA activities in their country and to read the rampant speculation in Europe of a likely military coup in the United States in response to Watergate and the Richard Nixon scandal. Remember Alexander Haig?)

Importantly, and fortunately, the relevant virtues for good citizens have never been limited to the elite or to the nation's leaders, nor to WASPs, and certainly not to any particular political party, religion, race or gender. Evidence of this assertion can be found in the millions of immigrants who arrived with nothing, yet who considered themselves blessed to be here and were eager to "live under [the United States'] protection ... demean themselves as good citizens [and give the United States] on all occasions their effectual support." These virtues have had a presence in the nation that cuts across all distinctions, including social class. (Although, it seems that it was always less so in New York City and more recently in several of the coastal metropolises.) The virtues are also closely allied with nationalism and a sense of national identity.

Also importantly, and unfortunately, egregious conduct that is clearly not the behavior of a "good citizen" is pretty common, whether criminal—such as stealing the neighbors' social security checks, filing fake income tax returns claiming refunds or engaging in Medicare fraud (whether by performing unnecessary procedures, at the risk of the patients, or simply submitting claims for procedures or services never performed)—or that simply seeks to avoid one's communal responsibilities, such as declining to work (at all or for more hours) in order to obtain governmental benefits. I have also become increasingly aware of how government contracts, programs and entitlements always tend to attract corrupt and fraudulent behavior.

So, even if most of the population is essentially law-abiding, an underlying question is how many free riders society can tolerate before it begins to breakdown. There will always be those who prefer to take the advantages provided by the sacrifices of others without making corresponding contributions, and society can tolerate a certain amount of such selfish behavior. Various societies make it more or less difficult to be a free rider. But, a point can be reached where the prevalence of free riders both strains the capabilities of the system and undermines the willingness of others to make the necessary sacrifices.

One of the biggest challenges for the United States today is how to create and maintain a sufficient number of good citizens. This issue is relevant to our social welfare policies, our tax policies and, of course, our immigration policies. (The first two categories seem more or less under control at this time, but the last is a national disgrace. Unfortunately, both parties have incentives to maintain the *status quo* on immigration. A fair and rational solution would deprive each of a powerful issue with some significant part of its constituencies.)

Effective moral authority presumably plays a role in the creation and maintenance of a successful percentage of good citizens. From where does such authority come and how is it promoted or created? Originally, moral authority was presumably based upon and enforced by a common religion and the civil characteristics promoted by that religion. In more modern times, moral authority must necessarily become more secular and more dependent on the setting of examples.

POLITICAL AND CIVIC LEADERSHIP

On the day of the funeral ceremony for George H.W. Bush in National Cathedral, the New York Times printed a column by one of its regulars, Ross Douthat, entitled: "Why We Miss the WASPs." NY*Times.com.*, Dec. 5, 2018. There were three points made that have stayed with me. First, despite what we now see as serious shortcomings, the WASP elite governed pretty wisely and pretty well. Second, the WASP elite voluntarily surrendered its position of leadership and moral authority, despite alternative options. And, third, its successors have not done as good a job.

As to the first point, the perceived shortcomings of WASPs were racism, certain moral intolerances or prejudices, relative emotional detachment and sexism. The strengths, in contrast, lay in the WASP commitment to the virtues of service, sacrifice, discipline, duty, honor, courage, self-restraint, civility and stoicism. These virtues were perceived to set a standard, one to be lived up to by the elite (and their children) and emulated or aspired to by others. They placed demands upon the members of the governing establishment, but they also set a standard by which people might judge themselves and others. And, the standard was broadly accepted, even if not regularly met.

These virtues have obvious benefits when it comes to governing. All one needs to do is to consider the result of the opposites: selfishness, greed, self-indulgence, self-dealing, whining and incivility. Where the governing elite embraces these opposites, you have a Nigeria, Congo, Malaysia, or Philippines (or the many other nations with governments known for corruption and exploitation). In addition to the benefits of being governed by a group that adheres to the WASP virtues (*e.g.*, less corruption, fraud, exploitation and deceit), the elite group's moral standing or authority and its ability to assert moral leadership are enhanced by such virtues as well. That was a clear win for the society and nation involved.

The second point is that sometime in the late '60s onward, the WASPs began to abandon voluntarily their position of moral authority. Curiously, when confronted with accusations of racism, sexism and political incorrectness, this elite, rather than fighting back, became increasingly introspective. Apparently, the WASPs' ability to empathize with those who had been discriminated against led first to embarrassment and then to a crisis of confidence. (At least, that is what I perceived in my family. I assume that the response of the "elite" was similar to that of the upper-middle class WASPs.)

The gradual withdrawal from moral leadership emboldened the critics to increase their attacks and their demands. Their positions became, in my mind, more extreme and went from credible and often persuasive to ludicrous; but, one could not reason with these critics, and attempts to do so invited being attacked as racist.

WASPs could have acknowledged the validity of some of the criticisms and undertaken steps to reform its behavior, while continuing to assert its moral authority. For example, there is nothing in the list of virtues that precludes more inclusiveness. Catholics and Jews and others had emulated the WASP values and enter the elite, families like the Kennedys and the Buckleys.

> "[A]n aristocratic spirit was transferable to a more diverse elite, that there could be Catholic and African-American and Jewish aristocrats – like, say, the family that has long stewarded this newspaper – who could adopt the WASP establishment's upper-class virtues without the ethnic and religious chauvinism."

Douthat, "The Case Against Meritocracy," NYTimes.com, December 8, 2018.

Of course, to have done so would have invited accusations of paternalism, elitism and prejudice. But, sometimes the right thing is to stand up and assert one's values.

The third point is that the new leadership has been less effective than the old. As to that, we have neither the length of experience nor the historical perspective to pass judgment. But, the early signs are not good.

Some commentators have recently been attracted to comparisons between today's leaders and Winston Churchill. For example, Bret Stephens writes:

> "'[Churchill] mobilized the English language and sent it into battle,' John F. Kennedy said (stealing a line from Edward Murrow) in awarding Churchill honorary United States citizenship in 1963. Of how many leaders now in office could that be said today – in any language?"

"An Antidote to Idiocy in 'Churchill'", NYTimes.com, December 14, 2018.

Churchill, like Washington and Lincoln, showed real leadership and asserted moral authority—the ability to inspire, to call forth from others strength, courage and determination. To repeat Stephens' question: Of how many leaders now in office could this be said today? There is certainly a lack moral authority among the political leaders at all levels of government today. But, is that really a change? Were the exceptional leaders of the past just that—exceptions?

And, Douthat continues:

> "[T]he meritocratic ideal ends up being just as undemocratic as the old emphasis on inheritance and tradition, and it forges an elite that has an aristocracy's vices (privilege, insularity, arrogance) without the sense of duty, self-restraint and noblesse oblige that WASPs at their best displayed. ...This spirit discourages inherited responsibility and cultural stewardship; it brushes away the disciplines of duty... ."

I have my doubts that meritocracy needs to be this way; but, even if Douthat is right, the appearance of a vacuum in today's political sphere is not surprising. The increasing emphasis has been on diversity, political correctness, multiculturalism and "correct" views on social issues like abortion and gay marriage. These concepts are insufficient bases for effective governing and certainly insufficient for the exercise of moral leadership.

It may be observed that the WASP elite was born into and lived lives of privilege, including material wellbeing. Thus, one might say, they did not need to view political positions as a way to make their fortunes (because they already had fortunes). If so, one might say there is a benefit of having a government run by individuals of privilege and property. Certainly, people who consider themselves as victims of the system, who are resentful or who seek reparations, compensation or revenge, are not very attractive prospects for leadership positions. The same is true of those who whine or complain, who are driven by envy or who are weak, timid and insecure.

So, should we limit government positions to persons of property and privilege? No. Being born to privilege is neither a guarantee of nor a requirement for having the virtues enumerated above. But, a love of country and community may be.

Consider two groups of potential leaders, one with the virtues of service, sacrifice, duty and courage, and the other with the characteristics of selfishness, self-dealing, political correctness, and personal cowardice (or a group of envious, resentful complainers seeking to get their "just deserts"). Which group would you want with you on the Titanic, on the battlefield of Gettysburg, in dark days of 1944 or on the morning after 9/11? Do these virtues matter to us only during times of great danger, or are they still relevant to the little challenges and crises of everyday existence.

THE DECLINE OF MORAL AUTHORITY

I do think that we have clearly experienced a deterioration in the level of moral authority and moral leadership in this country and around the world.

The key to the problem may be the word "authority". It bespeaks hierarchy. The recognition of virtue implies that some people are more virtuous than others, that there are distinctions of value among people, that some people are better people than others. Such views are contrary to the current emphasis on equality. We insist that all people are of equal worth; even though, they are obviously of widely differing abilities, skills and effectiveness, just as they are of different heights, weights, races and genders.

I perceived the shift as arising out of the civil rights movement and the challenges to racism in the 1960s. There followed the ideas of cultural and moral relativism. These concepts were not compelled by the rejection of racism; that moral worth is not a matter of race does not mean that degrees of moral worth do not exist. The concepts were more a matter of the growing emphasis on tolerance and inclusiveness and, of course, equality. There was also a trend increasingly to reject nationalism, carrying with it diminishing willingness to sacrifice for one's country.

There is evidence that this "problem" with authority (moral, cultural, religious, academic *etc.*) is now pervasive and fundamental, representing a major cultural shift. As a result, for example, the elite American educational institutions are in danger of failing to fulfill their fundamental responsibilities to preserve and promote the striving for knowledge, conservation of the past and the training of future leaders. The indispensable vigor of discourse and self-examination is being eroded by the demise of the "core curriculum" and distribution requirements, grade inflation and "pass/fail" courses, by the emphasis on inclusiveness and comfort (rather than independence and effort), by the increasingly expensive student amenities, limitations on speech, the creation of safe spaces and the erasure of memorials to the past that have unpleasant connotations.

Higher education should be hard and challenging, disruptive and provocative. It should require strenuous efforts and intense self-examination. Anthony Kronman, in *The Assault on American Excellence* (2019), argues that the goal of elite education "is to preserve, transmit and honor an *aristocratic* tradition of respect for human greatness." (Emphasis added.) The premise, once taken as a given, is "that there is such a thing as character; that a person's character can be better or worse; that character is shaped by education; and that one of the goals of higher education is to instill in the student a love of those things for which a person of fine character should care." *Id.*[2]

The problem in the academy, in my view, is the lack of courage and commitment on the part of the academic leadership. In part this is a result, like with the WASP elite, of empathy (and embarrassment) leading to deference and then to the undermining of the strength of conviction in the core values of the academy. In part, it is a result of pandering to students to succeed in the highly competitive process of attracting the "best" applicant and in securing the highest rating from the media. The institutions have become increasingly businesses catering to their "customers" rather than beacons of excellence attracting those willing to accept the challenge and make the commitment.

So, there has been a decline of political, academic and religious leadership, bringing a general decline in moral authority. One result is the failure to perceive anyone as setting an example for the rest of us to follow. Who do we now admire or look up to? Is there anybody?

Our cultural heroes?

I was raised on *The Lone Ranger*, *Bonanza* and *Gunsmoke*—on Ben, Adam, Hoss, Little Joe and Matt Dillon. It was a time of innocence, of self-restraint (or self-denial, in today's terminology), the era of the "strong silent type", as reflected in Toby Keith's 1993 song, "Should've been a cowboy":

> "I bet you've never heard ol' Marshal Dillon say Miss Kitty, have you ever thought of runnin' away? ...They never tied the knot, his heart wasn't in it He just stole a kiss as he rode away He never hung his hat up at Kitty's place"

But, today? Our heroes appear to be reality show stars, YouTube and Twitter sensations, professional celebrities and anyone who can "earn" at least $10 million a year without actually producing anything. If these personalities represent our new societal standards and aspirations, what is the consequence for the country?

THE DECLINE OF VIRTUE

Winston Churchill wrote:

> "the behavior of the male passengers [on the Titanic] reflects nothing but honour upon our civilization. . . . I cannot help feeling proud of our race and its traditions as proved by this event. Boatloads of women and children tossing on the sea safe and sound—and the rest—silence. Honour to their memory. . . . How differently imperial Rome or Ancient Greece would have settled the problem. The swells, the potentates would have gone off with their concubines and pet slaves and soldier guards. . . . whoever could bribe the crew would have had the preference and the rest

could go to hell. But such ethics could neither build Titanics with science nor lose them with honour."

Lance Morrow, "Did Chivalry Go Down With the Titanic?", *WSJ.com*, December 14, 2018.

Churchill spoke of "our race" and "our civilization", of course; but, his focus was upon the acts, not the color or religion, of the men on board the Titanic. The acts of a person are not determined by race, religion, gender or sexual orientation, but by what we have called "character."

Higher standards could have been expected of much of the community, despite the failings of our political leadership. Remember the words of George Washington, the United States "requires only that they who live under its protection should demean themselves as good citizens, in giving it on all occasions their effectual support." All that is required is commitment, loyalty and sacrifice. Or, as John F. Kennedy famously said in his inaugural address in 1961: "Ask not what your country can do for you--ask what you can do for your country."

But, that has not happened. Instead, these virtues have rapidly crumbled as the aspirational norm for American education and society. Many have lamented the decline in service, duty, honor, courage and civility. Unfortunately, the loss of these individual virtues seems to be most marked among the highly educated, multicultural urban elite, who seem to have more in common with their similarly situated colleagues around the globe than with their fellow citizens at home.

How would today's political values look to

> *"a 1960s Democrat. Those liberals were patriots who loved America and would have had no use for people who see only its misdeeds. They stood up for what was right and had an exhilarating confidence in American justice and greatness. They knew the country had problems, but also knew we could solve them."*

F.H. Buckley, "Trump May Be the True Liberal," *WSJ.com*, January 1, 2019.

To what is this change attributable?

Lance Morrow goes on to ask:

> *"Would the social evolutions of the past century, including recent politics of gender, have any bearing on the behavior of men*

> *and women and on the life-or-death choices they made on the deck of a sinking ship? . . . In the absence of the old gentility—under which men were expected to hold the door for women, to rise when they entered the room, and to give up their seats in lifeboats—would the simpler principle of dog-eat-dog assert itself? ...Is it possible that the doctrine of equality has, among other things, relieved the male of his duty to behave like a gentleman and left him free to be a cad?"*

"Did Chivalry Go Down With the Titanic?", WSJ.com, December 14, 2018.

From my standpoint, the initial inflection point came in the late 1960s with the slogan "better Red than dead," a sentiment that deeply shocked my parent's generation. A slightly later but similar slogan, "make love, not war," seemed like a modern and decadent version of the Greek comedy Lysistrata, using the carrot rather than the stick to end war—offering more fun and less sacrifice for everyone. (Sometimes, the more appropriate "make peace, not war" was used.) Despite strong desires for a more just and peaceful world, there was the emergence of a strong "me" philosophy, particularly among the better educated and more cosmopolitan. That is not to say that my generation did not do many good deeds, especially in the spirit of humanitarianism. But, the changes in the national values accelerated in this new century, leading to today's "identity politics" and, with it, the dismissal of personal responsibility.

Probably the most significant societal changes underlying all of this has been the increasing rejection of religion and religious teaching and the increasing reliance on the State as the potential solution to all problems.

This phenomenon was described in a recent speech by Attorney General William P. Barr:

> *"... this idea of the State as the alleviator of bad consequences has given rise to a new moral system that goes hand-in-hand with the secularization of society. ...Christianity teaches a micro-morality. We transform the world by focusing on our own personal morality and transformation. The new secular religion teaches macro-morality. One's morality is not gauged by their private conduct, but rather on their commitment to political causes and collective action... ."*

"Remarks to the Law School and the de Nicola Center for Ethics and Culture at the University of Notre Dame," U.S. *Department of Justice*, October 11, 2019.

Although this speech has been much maligned by the media, I think that it is hard not to accept that Barr's observation captures something important about what has happened. It represents the decline of individual virtue as a guiding principle and an emphasis, instead, upon collective responses to perceived inequities and injustices. One may think that good, but not that it did not happen. I find it also hard to dispute the conclusion that while Government programs have ameliorated some of the consequences of bad decisions, destructive life styles and unequal opportunities; they have done little to address the underlying causes and may have actually exacerbated some of the problems. (This argument is continued in the next chapter.) Where there is ample room for fair debate is the question of what to do now. Will more Government involvement finally eliminate the problems? Would reduced Government involvement improve the situation? Are there other alternatives?

THE DECLINE OF HEROES

And now, the vigorous efforts to denigrate and erase major historical figures because they had flaws currently deemed unacceptable. All humans have flaws and imperfections. We are bundles of strengths and weaknesses. Different cultures appear to rank flaws (and strengths) differently. Some defects (and strengths) are prioritized over others. Today, shockingly to me, cowardice, greed and self-centeredness are forgivable. Racism and sexism are not, even when existing at a time when those attitudes were the "norm". At the same time, the courage to act, the ability to achieve and independence from the crowd are overlooked.

Is there not much that is admirable in Stonewall Jackson and Robert E. Lee, despite the side on which they fought? Indeed, should we not be impressed by the courage shown by Lee in facing his terrible choice between the Union and his home state of Virginia, by the fact that he made a decision based on his sense of honor (whether right or wrong) and that he bore the consequences of his choice fully and with dignity?

The "renaming movement" not only removes the heroes from our worldview, It misleadingly suggests that the monuments were erected for the flaws, not the men. And, it threatens to diminish our recognition of the fundamental fact of moral ambiguity (and complexity), to cheapen (and disguise) the important history of civilization's faltering efforts to be better and more just. Is that what we want?

> "Are we really so faint of heart that we can no longer bear to allow the honoring of great men of the past who fail in some respects to meet our current specifications? It's true that all three men held either slaves or racist beliefs. Does that exhaust everything we need to know about them? Ought it to outweigh the value of everything else they did?"

Wilfred M. McClay, "The Weaponization of History," WSJ.com, August 25, 2019.

So, there is no one to admire; only those to whom we do not object.

Ultimately, what do we need in political leaders? Is bland inoffensiveness preferable to vigor, with all its flaws? But, how could it ever really be sufficient? Where would we be without those who act and do so bravely, accepting the consequences? Those who actually grapple with the grubby, messy world in which we live, rather than just complain about it.

Teddy Roosevelt famously asserted:

> "It is not the critic who counts; not the man who points out how the strong man stumbles, or where the doer of deeds could have done them better. The credit belongs to the man who is actually in the arena, whose face is marred by dust and sweat and blood; who strives valiantly; who errs, who comes short again and again, ... but who does actually strive to do the deeds... ."

Do we still believe these words are relevant or have they been relegated to the historical trashcan as an example of patronizing elitism? Is the critic or the complainer now king? Do we no longer admire and salute those who "actually strive to do the deeds"? Have we lost all common sense?

THE ROLE OF COMMUNITY

Leadership is essential, but only part of it can come from the political arena. In fact, it may be that national political leadership does not make much difference, at least, not directly. What we need is persons in all areas to be leaders and decision-makers, setting standards and serving as examples. Is it not possible, or even likely, that it is family, community, church and other associations that make the real difference?

The layers between family and national government can be most important, what Timothy Carney calls the "middle". Carney argues that the sense of community comes from participation in associations, particularly churches but also sports teams, social clubs, volunteer organizations, the PTA, *etc*. It is these associations of people that, he claims, foster civil society. *Alienated America* (2019). When they wither, the (physical) communities themselves die, as does the sense of community. So, maybe what we need to do is promote communities and try to increase the sense of community.

A recent opinion column noted, in a specific context, the potential effectiveness of local leadership and local sources of moral authority:

> *"Hillary Clinton pointed the way in her book 'It Takes a Village.' Of course, once you move past her title, Mrs. Clinton's village turns out to depend on federal bureaucrats. But the principle [of the title] is worth rescuing. ... [F]ar from empowering ... local leaders to act when they spot trouble—teachers, scoutmasters, pastors, police chiefs, shopkeepers, coaches—we have spent the past half century undermining their authority."*

William McGurn, "Guns and the Do-Something Fallacy," WSJ.com, August 12, 2019.

Certainly, good citizens are mainly found in communities, acting as good neighbors, as volunteers in a wide range of community activities, as the bulwark of protection against the hostile world beyond. The heart of good citizenship is participation in the life of the community and, by extension, the country. The hallmark of such good citizenship is the sense of individual responsibility both for the well-being of that community and for the well-being of the country.

Let me repeat a question I ask above about leaders: Consider two groups, one with the virtues of service, sacrifice, duty and courage, and the other with the characteristics of selfishness, self-dealing, political correctness, and personal cowardice (or a group of envious, resentful complainers seeking to get their 'just deserts'). Which group would you want in your community or as your neighbor?

THE FUTURE?

So, where to now? How do we support and sustain communities? Or, families? Is it the responsibility of, or even a proper (or feasible) role for, government, whether local or national or international? In the end, is it not just a matter of participation? And, does that not depend upon individuals and the exercise of their capacity for relationships? Perhaps, the moral underpinnings of the nation can be slowly recaptured by the people. But, does that require a renewed nationalism? It is easy to be melodramatic (or sanctimonious) about these subjects. The challenge is to figure out what, if anything, to do. Are the old traditional values simply lost forever? If not, how can they be revived? If so, can something constructive be created in their place? And, how can that happen? A people (and each person) needs something that commands loyalty, whether it be a nation state, a religion or a brother/sisterhood with a code of honor. Yet, I do not see how we go back to the past. So, we need something forward-looking that inspires and elicits commitment and a willingness to sacrifice. What could that be for today's secular, multi-cultural, multi-national, cosmopolitan elite? Or, are they as a group simply a lost cause? If so, then the prospects of a more global and inclusive community seem bleak.

Endnotes

[1] "Letter to the Jews of Newport", 18 August 1790, *Washington Papers*, 6:284-85.

[2] While I largely agree with what Korrman says about the symptoms of the disease, I largely disagree with him about the causes. I do not think that an emphasis on vocational training is part of the problem. There is a need and a valid place for vocational education. And, the eroding culture at a Harvard, Yale or Amherst College is not a result of a growing emphasis on job training. I also disagree that the humanities hold any exclusive claims with respect to the study of the deeper questions about existence and meaning. Those issues arise in the serious study of any subject. And, I disagree that careers and ambition are inconsistent with an acute awareness of the issues of meaning and morals. Indeed, I think that grappling with action in the face of the realities of our messy, complex and ambiguous world gives a special poignancy to such issues.

A Note on "Systemic Racism"

Racism can be ugly, especially when coupled with hatred, or anger, or fear. But, racism is also personal. People are racists. Racism is a matter of beliefs, feelings, attitudes and intentions, as well as of behavior. So, there are serious limits to what government can do about racism. Government can prohibit and combat various racist actions (like "hate crimes" or job discrimination), but not racism itself. Churches, families, maybe schools, possibly communities, but not government.

This country has a long history of discriminatory behavior—exclusion, hostility, violence and, often, compelled residential segregation—based on differences among people, whether racial or other. Such discrimination has affected Native Americans, Irish, Italians (especially, Southern Italians), Polish, Chinese, Japanese, Hispanics, Jews, and so on. (In many cases, discrimination was effected by official government action as well as private conduct.) Racists are a blemish on our society (and are present in most others).

I applaud the affirmation by communities and churches of the country's founding principles and the recent reinvigoration of the efforts fully to realize them. Those efforts are for the good of all. And, it is a worthy objective for each of us to recognize our own biases and prejudices, including racial biases. Some other reactions, however, are destructive. We badly need acceptance, tolerance and good will, and not just between races.

Now, we are talking about "systemic [or institutional or structural] racism". Generally, in ordinary usage, institutions could not be racist. They may have discriminatory consequences and their founders or leaders may have been (or may be) racists, but not the institutions. But, we now have a new definition: "Racism: The marginalization and/or oppression of people of color based on a socially constructed racial hierarchy that privileges white people." ADL (The "Anti-Defamation League", founded in 1913 to combat anti-semitism), July 2020. *See also*, John McWhorter, "The Dictionary Definition of Racism Has to Change," *The Atlantic*, June 22, 2020

("If I had it my way ... we would allow that racism now refers to a societal state, and revive prejudice to refer to attitudinal bias").

Some refer to systemic racism as "white privilege," but that is nonsense—it is not about anyone's privilege, but about someone's disadvantage. ("White privilege" is not based on Black, or minority, oppression.) Moreover, it is not only whites (or only white Protestants) that can be racist. I was fortunate to grow up in a two-parent household, to have caring and supportive parents, to live in a community sufficiently isolated that it was safe for children to walk themselves to school or roam the neighborhood. I was also fortunate to be tall. In all of these things, I was lucky; in none of them, was I "privileged." So, the phrase is to me a misnomer. It is not "white privilege," but the allegedly racially discriminatory effects of our history and our current system that should be the current focus.

This is a curious development. The social and moral opprobrium traditionally ascribed to racism is not appropriate for institutions or systems that happen to cause negative effects on "persons of color". So, the new emphasis would seem to reduce the seriousness of the characterization (which McWhorter would now call "prejudice"). But, it does play to the sensibilities of those who think that government benefits are the solution to most problems.

At the same time as this new concern with "systemic racism", the degree of violence and group lawlessness has increased dramatically. For example: "Neighborhoods in some of the largest US cities erupted in gun violence over the Fourth of July weekend [2020}, killing an estimated 160 people and leaving more than 500 wounded from Friday night to Sunday." "Gun violence kills 160 as holiday weekend exposes tale of 'two Americas'," *The Guardian*, 7 July 2020.

And, one month later:

> "On Friday [Portland] police said 'people defied orders to disperse and threw rocks, frozen or hard-boiled eggs and commercial-grade fireworks at officers,' the Associated Press reports. Rioters also 'filled pool noodles with nails and placed them in the road, causing extensive damage to a patrol vehicle.' On Saturday night, arsonists set a fire inside the Portland police union building and rioters outside landed two officers in the hospital. ...Meanwhile in Chicago on Sunday night, hundreds of looters ransacked stores along the Magnificent Mile. ... The Chicago Tribune reports that some looters 'could be seen throw-

ing merchandise into rental trucks and other large vehicles before driving away.' ...13 cops were injured."

The Editorial Board, "Mayhem Continues, Protest Narrative Crumbles: Looters rampage in Chicago and arson returns in Portland," WSJ.com, August 10, 2020.

It is not politically correct to refer to these recent events as "riots", so we will say that during a period of widespread racial protests, there has been murder, arson, violence and looting. (Contrary to some recent claims, incidents of racial violence in 1917 in East St. Louis; in 1919 in Chicago, Omaha and several other American cities; in 1921 in Tulsa, as well as at seaports across the United Kingdom, were referred to as "riots" and were generally condemned by government officials. These riots with whites attacking blacks were largely motivated, however, not by racism, but by competition over jobs following WW I.)

The year 2020 also saw a huge increase in homicides:

"This year, 51 cities of various sizes across the U.S. saw an average 35% jump in murder from 2019 to 2020 – a 'historically awful' development, says New Orleans-based crime analyst Jeff Asher, who crunched those numbers. A different study looking at 21 U.S. cities found 610 more murders in those jurisdictions this year over last year. In those cities, gun assaults increased by 10% over 2019."

"2020's murder increase is 'unprecedented.' But is it a blip?", *The Christian Science Monitor*, December 14, 2020.

The year 2021 was only worse.

"SYSTEMIC RACISM"?

What are the particular institutions today that have racially discriminatory effects? And, what specifically are their problem features?

One view was recently set forth by Raphael Bostic, the President of the Federal Reserve Bank of Atlanta, in a July 2020 Bank release:

"[M]any of our fellow citizens endure the burden of unjust, exploitative, and abusive treatment by institutions in this country.

> [T]he examples of such institutionalized racism are many, and include slavery, federal law (consider the Three- Fifths Compromise our founding fathers established to determine federal representation), sanctioned intimidation during Reconstruction, Jim Crow laws in southern states, redlining by bankers and brokers, segregation, voter suppression, and racial profiling in policing."

He continues: "...To be fair, we have made some progress."

Some progress?

Bostic's list of examples of "institutional racism" are things from the distant past. Except for "racial profiling", the extent and effects of which are debatable (and discussed below), all of the things listed were banned between 50 and 150 years ago (by the Acts listed in the history set out below), all long since gone from the system. Moreover, some were not racist (like the Three-Fifths Compromise) and others were not institutional. His is simply not a useful nor informative list.

The question here is what are the actual institutional examples of discriminatory effects? Where do we look for an answer?

Much of the publicity for the claim came from the "1619 Project", an effectively rebutted piece of purported history, and an attempted revival of Derek Bell's "critical race theory", also largely discredited (obviously, some/many may disagree with my judgment on "critical race theory"). The public commentary is not very helpful. For example, McWhorter says "one might say that societal racism is to blame for neighborhoods with decaying infrastructure, because white flight lowered tax revenues." "The Dictionary Definition of Racism Has to Change," *The Atlantic*, June 22, 2020. Is that really a meaningful statement? Does it shed light either on the causes of the problems or on possible solutions?

Some approaches effectively define racial inequality as racism. Ibram X. Kendi, in his 2019 best seller *How To Be An Antiracist*, includes in racism the failure to oppose policies that result in racial inequalities (which he calls "racial inequities"): less wealth, lower income, poorer health, shorter life expectancy, less home ownership, *etc*. The problem with such a single-minded focus on the impact on racial groups is not that such impact is irrelevant, but that it is uni-dimensional. Real public policy issues and actions are necessarily multi-dimensional and must be so evaluated. Moreover, inequality is not necessarily inequity. In many cases, unequal may be very equitable.

Recent attention has largely become focused not on attitudes or intent or on actual racism, but on the lingering effects from past events in our history. So, the concern presumably is primarily for the effects on American-born Blacks descended from slaves—not first or second generation immigrants who are black or brown, but blacks who are American-born of American-born parents. These are the people who would bear the scars of our history of slavery. That category would include Condoleezza Rice, Martin Luther King, Jr., and Thurgood Marshall; but, it would not include Barrack Obama, Kamala Harris or Colin Powell. It is not a matter of race, but of ancestry and cultural heritage. Or, the logic says that it should be.

Shelby Steele asserts that: "'Systemic racism' is a term that tries to recover authenticity for a less and less convincing black identity. This racism is really more compensatory than systemic. It was invented to make up for the increasing absence of the real thing." "The Inauthenticity Behind Black Lives Matter," WSJ.com, November 22, 2020. It is clearly being advanced to support "compensatory" and preferential treatment.

For example, The state of Oregon has established a Covid relief fund exclusively for blacks and black-owned businesses, so Hispanic businesses in similar distress are denied relief on the basis of race.

> *"'Centuries of systemic and institutional discrimination—perpetuated and exacerbated by current systems—have caused economic disparities.' ... [The relief] is available* **not on the basis of discrimination against applicants but on the presumption that all blacks and black businesses have been discriminated against by the state."**

James Huffman, "Oregon's Segregated Covid Relief Fund Is Blatantly Unconstitutional," WSJ.com, December. 4, 2020 (emphasis added).

The concept of "systemic racism" suggests that any identifiable disadvantages of Blacks today must be attributed to or blamed on the "system". (Of course, racist attitudes exist toward many other groups beyond Blacks.) A recent letter to the editor of the Wall Street Journal (Maggie Reeves, October 13, 2020.) asked the pertinent question:

> *"I wonder what reasons ... exist for racial disparities in our society other than racial prejudice? The 'black underclass' and 'black elites' both want safe neighborhoods and better schools for themselves, their families, and their communities."*

The writer clearly intended the question to be rhetorical only. But, it is, in fact, a real question, and it is one that demands a real answer.

A Brief History of Slavery

The treatment of humans as property or chattel slavery has been an ancient and almost universal practice. "Slavery and the slave trade had been global phenomena for centuries by the early 17th century, involving Europeans and non-Europeans as slave traders and the enslaved." Bret Stephens, "1619 Chronicles: Journalism does better when it writes the first rough draft of history, not the last word on it," *The New York Times*, October 9, 2020.

It was generally based not on race but on kinship or identity and mainly arose out of military conquest. Slave trading and slave traders are also of long and disparate lineages. To some extent, supply created demand; and the existence of slavery in a society had economic consequences that promoted its continuation.

> *"Most human beings need a good deal of care and resources, and can usually be considered a net economic loss until they are twelve or sometimes fifteen years old. It rarely makes economic sense to breed slaves—which is why, globally, slaves have so often been the product of military aggression... ."*

David Graeber and David Wengrow, *The Dawn of Everything* (2021), p.188.

The first slaves in the Americas were captives of indigenous peoples in Central and South America. In North America, the indigenous peoples of the Pacific Northwest had slaves.

> *"[[A]ccounts suggest that perhaps a quarter of the indigenous Northwest Coast population lived in bondage—which is about equivalent to proportions found in the Roman Empire, or classical Athens, or indeed the cotton plantations of the American South. What's more , slavery on the Northwest Coast was a hereditary status: if you were a slave, your children were also fated to be so."*

Id., p.185.

African slaves were brought to the New World in the first two decades of the 16th century, specifically to South America and the Caribbean.

> "Slavery existed in parts of Africa before the fifteenth century, but with the advent of the transatlantic trade in enslaved Africans, abductions and inter-ethnic conflicts greatly increased in West Africa as local chiefs responded to the immense demand from European slave traders. ...[T]here appears to be a substantial gap in levels of interpersonal trust between areas affected by the slave trade and those that were spared... ."

Oded Galor, *The Journey of Humanity: The Origins of Wealth and Inequality* (2022), pp.173-4.

Almost all Africans sold into slavery were sold by other Africans. Of the estimated 25 million Africans so sold, more than half went to the Middle East. The largest number of slaves from the trans-Atlantic trade went to Brazil, the second largest number went to the Caribbean. Only some 300,000 out of 10.5 million successfully transported to the New World came directly to North America. Most of the slaves in the United States were brought from the Caribbean, already having been slaves there. Hakim Adi, "Africa and the Transatlantic Slave Trade," BBC, updated 5 October 2012.

In the English colonies of North America, the first slaves arrived in 1619. But, that event was, in fact, a mere accident: "The Africans who arrived in Virginia that August ended up there only because they had been seized by English privateers from a Portuguese ship headed for the port of Veracruz in Mexico." Stephens, "1619 Chronicles," *The New York Times*, October 9, 2020.

"[U]p to the end of the eighteenth century, the heart of the plantation economy was French and British." Thomas Piketty, *A Brief History of Equality* (2022), p.68.

> "In the 1780s, the French slaveholding islands held the largest concentration of slaves in the Euro-American world—about 700,000—compared with 600,000 in the British possessions, and 500,000 on the plantations in the southern United States. ...[T]hese were truly slave islands, in the sense that the proportion of slaves rose as high as 90 percent of the total population ...in the 1780s (or even 95 percent if we include free Blacks and métis, those of mixed-race descent). ...In comparison, during the same period slaves represented ... [30-35] percent of the popula-

> tion of the southern United States and [50% in] Brazil, and the available sources suggest comparable proportions in Athens and in Rome in antiquity."

Id., pp.68-69.

The demand for slave labor in the Caribbean had grown with the cultivation of sugar cane. The demand in the United States exploded in the early 1800s with the cultivation of cotton, replacing tobacco on much acreage. *The Lowcountry Digital History Initiative* ("LDHI").

The slavery question was a disruptive controversy from the beginning of the nation. A compromise was reached to enable the formation of a union, with the expectation of many that slavery would die out.

The U.S. Constitution does not endorse or accept slavery and does not use the word "slave" (or "slavery"):

> "The Migration or Importation of such Persons as any of the States now existing shall think proper to admit shall not be prohibited by the Congress prior to the Year one thousand eight hundred and eight, but a Tax or duty may be imposed on such Importation, not exceeding ten dollars for each Person."

Article 1, Section 9.

> "Representatives and direct Taxes shall be apportioned among the several States which may be included within this Union, according to their respective Numbers, which shall be determined by adding to the whole Number of free Persons, including those bound to Service for a Term of Years, and excluding Indians not taxed, three fifths of all other Persons."

Article I, Section 2.

The "other Persons" were not "free Persons," i.e., they were slaves. This provision was a compromise, and it limited the political influence of the Southern states where the slaves were located. It would have been more anti-slavery not to count "other Persons" at all, but the provision was a compromise. "Indians not taxed" were considered to be members of other nations.

The slave trade into the U.S. had been inactive from the 1770s until early 1800. Legal restrictions and taxes were imposed starting in 1794. The United States outlawed the importation of slaves in 1807, effective 1808. (The U.K. also banned the slave trade later in 1807.) Thus, until 1800,

> *"none of the states had reopened the African trade.... Before 1800 all introductions into the U.S. were thus illegal, even if the slaves were brought in by foreign ships. After 1800, however, Georgia and South Carolina reopened their international slave trade, and in the next eight years, these two states would introduce about 100,000 new slaves from Africa."*

"Abolition of the Slave Trade," *abolition.nypl.org*, 2020.

The domestic slave exchange continued, however. It was, for example, big business in Alexandria, Virginia (part of the District of Columbia from 1789 to 1847), facilitating the reallocation of slaves from the Deep South, many ending up in Virginia. These slave exchanges were profitable businesses, generating several large personal fortunes. Thus, the vast preponderance of slaves in the United States in 1860 had been born here. Many were third generation Americans.

The Missouri Compromise was enacted in 1820, limiting the extension of slavery in the Western territories. Then, setbacks occurred in the 1850s with both Congress (the repeal of the Missouri compromise) and the Supreme Court (the *Dred Scott* decision). The subsequent Civil War resulted in 750,000 deaths (2% of the population) and cost $5.2 billion (greater than the GDP of 1860). Slavery was ended, but at great expense.

The wealth of the 20th century United States is not the result of slavery. By the mid-19th century, manufacturing was already beginning to challenge agriculture as the main economic activity. The Civil War very greatly accelerated the process. The North prospered; the South suffered a catastrophic economic decline.

Subsequent events included: The Emancipation Proclamation in 1863, the 13th Amendment in 1865, the 14th Amendment in 1868, and the 15th Amendment in 1870. (Note, the 19th Amendment, giving women the vote, was only ratified in 1920.) But, there was another step backwards, following the Hayes vs. Tilden election of 1876. It is called "The Compromise of 1877."

> *"The Compromise of 1877 was an informal agreement between southern Democrats and allies of the Republican Rutherford Hayes to settle the result of the 1876 presidential election and marked the end of the Reconstruction era. ...The Democrats*

> agreed not to block Hayes' victory on the condition that Republicans withdraw all federal troops from the South ... [which] effectively ended the Reconstruction era. ...[P]romises to protect civil and political rights of blacks were not kept, and the end of federal interference in southern affairs led to widespread disenfranchisement of blacks voters."

History.com, March 17, 2011 (updated November 27, 2019).

Nonetheless:

> "The progress of blacks from the Civil War to World War II, in some respects was fairly rapid because ...Blacks were just overwhelmingly impoverished. By the time of World War II, however, you saw the beginnings, the crystallization of a black class structure. ... You saw the development of a growing working class population, so much so that they probably represented at that time about 25 percent of the black population. And you saw a dwindling number of truly lower class blacks."

Ben Wattenberg, *The First Measured Century* on PBS: *The Other Way of Looking at American History*,"William Julius Wilson Interview," 2000.

And:

> "[WW II] opened up job opportunities in factories because of the labor shortage, and blacks experienced fairly rapid mobility during that time. And it also ... hastened their entry into blue-collar positions.... I'm talking about factory jobs in urban areas, even in Southern cities blacks were working, particularly in those factories in the South and urban areas that were producing war machinery."

PBS, "Interview of William Julius Wilson by Henry Louis 'Skip' Gates, Jr.," *Frontline*, November 2015.

Further Federal government actions sought to reduce discrimination:

>> Executive Order 9981 (desegregating the military) 1948
>> *Brown v. Bd. of Education* 1954
>> The Civil Rights Act of 1964
>> The Voting Rights Act of 1965
>> The Fair Housing Act of 1968
>> The Hate Crimes Prevention Act of 1999

The Hate Crimes Prevention Act of 2009

The existence of slavery in North America in the 1770s is no surprise. It had spread from the Spanish and Portuguese colonies to the English colonies in the Americas over the prior 150 years. Slavery carried over from colonial days posed a significant challenge for the United States over much of its history, but a challenge that the Nation has largely overcome.

That is a history of which we should be proud, not ashamed, because of what followed 1776.

> "...[A] politically formidable 'defining contradiction' 'that all men are created equal' — came into existence through the Declaration of Independence. ... As for the notion that the Declaration's principles were 'false' in 1776, ideals aren't false merely because they are unrealized, much less because many of the men who championed them, and the nation they created, hypocritically failed to live up to them. Most of us, at any given point in time, are falling short of some ideal we nonetheless hold to be true or good."

Bret Stephens, "1619 Chronicles," *The New York Times*, October 9, 2020.

RACIST LAW ENFORCEMENT?

Racial discrimination in the enforcement of laws is unacceptable and a clear violation of our principles. The first question is whether there is evidence of significant (not isolated) acts of such racial discrimination. If so, then the second question would be whether that evidence reflects the presence of actual racism or the results of existing systems or structures.

Discrimination

On this first question, the data is incomplete and unclear.

Take fatal police shootings. For 2017-9, white deaths from police shootings averaged 407 per year and black deaths, 222 per year:

> "Victims were majority white (52%) but disproportionately black (32%) with a fatality rate 2.8 times higher among blacks than whites. Most victims were reported to be armed (83%); however,

> black victims were more likely to be unarmed (14.8%) than white (9.4%) or Hispanic (5.8%) victims."

Sarah DeGue, Katherine A. Fowler, and Cynthia Calkins, "Deaths Due to Use of Lethal Force by Law Enforcement: Findings From the National Violent Death Reporting System, 17 U.S. States, 2009–2012," *Am. J. Prev. Med.*, November 2016.

And,

> "Among all groups, black men and boys face the highest lifetime risk of being killed by police. Our models predict that about 1 in 1,000 black men and boys will be killed by police over the life course (96 per 100,000). ...Latino men and boys have an estimated risk of being killed by police of about 53 per 100,000, ...while white men and boys face a lifetime risk of about 39 per 100,000."

Frank Edwards, Hedwig Lee, and Michael Esposito, "Risk of being killed by police use of force in the United States by age, race–ethnicity, and sex," *PNAS*, August 20, 2019.

But, Blacks had much more frequent encounters with police. When adjustments are made for that factor, the disparity almost disappears: "we find no racial differences in officer-involved shootings...." Roland G. Fryer, Jr., "An Empirical Analysis of Racial Differences in Police Use of Force," *law.yale.edu*, July 2016. Similarly:

> "A Black person in America is roughly three times more likely than a white person to be killed by police. ...In 2018, the rate of arrests for violent crime was 3.6 times higher for Black people than white people. So actually, the argument goes, Black people are underrepresented as victims of police killings, after controlling for the number of encounters... . "

Aubrey Clayton, "The statistical paradox of police killings: In the numbers of fatal encounters with the cops, one kind of discrimination masks another," *Boston Globe*, June 11, 2020.

However, Clayton persuasively argues: "The inflated number of nonlethal encounters Black people experience due to racial profiling could be what shifts the balance, perversely using one kind of discrimination, overpolicing, to mask another: *the greater use of deadly force against Black suspects.*" *Id* (emphasis in original).

"[C]ould be"? Well, yes, it could be. But, is it?

For 2018, an analysis showed that of all persons arrested, 69% were white and 27% were black; of arrests for violent crimes, the percentages were 58% and 38%. So, blacks (13% of the population) were twice as likely to be arrested as whites and 3 times as likely to be arrested for a violent crime. For murder and manslaughter, blacks represented 53% (more than 4 times as likely as whites). U.S Department of Justice, OJJDP *Statistical Briefing Book*, "Estimated number of arrests by offense and race, 2018," October 31, 2019. For curfew and loitering offenses, blacks represented 56% (over 4 times as likely as whites), but for drunkenness, disorderly conduct and vagrancy, blacks were between 25% and 30% (2 times as likely or less). *Id.*

However, at the same time, "[for] non-lethal uses of force – putting hands on civilians (which includes slapping or grabbing) or pushing individuals into a wall or onto the ground, there are large racial differences. In the raw data, blacks and Hispanics are more than fifty percent more likely to have an interaction with police which involves any use of force." Roland G. Fryer, Jr., "An Empirical Analysis of Racial Differences in Police Use of Force," *law.yale.edu*, July 2016.

Are black law-breakers just more likely to be caught? Probably not, but the question is hard to answer empirically. Yet, we can answer whether the rates of crime are the same in communities independent of racial characteristics? That answer is an unambiguous "no."

In fact, "the proportion of black suspects arrested by the police tends to match closely the proportion of offenders identified as black by victims in the [FBI's] National Crime Victimization Survey." Patrick Worral, "Do black Americans commit more crime?" *Channel 4 News*, Factcheck, 27 November 2014. Moreover, it is likely that Black communities under report crime, so the actual statistics could be even more adverse for Black communities. The same conclusions were reached in the most recent study using the same sources of data:

> "Based on the 2018 NCVS and UCR, black people accounted for 29% of violent-crime offenders and 35% of violent-crime offenders in incidents reported to police, compared to 33% of all persons arrested for violent crimes. ...Among the most serious incidents of violent crime (rape or sexual assault, robbery, and aggravated assault), there were **no statistically significant differ-**

ences by race between offenders identifed in the NCVS and persons arrested per the UCR."

U.S. Department of Justice, Office of Justice Programs, Bureau of Justice Statistics, "Race and Ethnicity of Violent Crime Offenders and Arrestees, 2018," January 2021 (emphasis added).

Similarly suggestive: "According to the CDC, about 14,500 Americans were murdered with guns in 2017. More than half were young black men killed in metro areas, which has been the pattern for at least the last five years... " Melissa Chan, "How Likely Is the Risk of Being Shot in America? It Depends," *Time*, August 16, 2019.

Thus, a black man was 7 times more likely than a white man to be killed by a gun and, generally, by other black men. So, while Blacks are 3 times more likely to be killed by police than whites, they are 7 times more likely to be killed by guns.

The crime rates by neighborhood evidence racial disparities as well.

> *"African Americans and Hispanics are more likely to be victims of violent crimes — especially serious violent crimes — than are whites, although the gap has narrowed over the past 10 years... . African Americans are disproportionately victims of homicide compared with whites or Hispanics. Similarly, low-income people are much more likely than others to experience crime, including violent crime."*

"Neighborhoods and Violent Crime," *Office of Policy Development and Research*, Summer 2016. (However, the differences are not as great as one might expect.)

I note that there is a similar racial pattern in high school disciplinary actions. "Black women were three times as likely as white women to say they'd been disciplined." Mellisa Korn, "College Common App Drops Question About Discipline, Citing Racial Disparities," WSJ.com, September 20, 2020. (This data is for high school students applying to college. The solution adopted is to remove the question from the application. But, the cause of the pattern is not addressed. I think that the fact of such a disparity is more alarming than any possible obstacle to college admissions that the question–or the answers–present.)

More broadly, "[a] U.S. Government Accountability Oversight report from 2018 shows Black students accounted for 15.5% of all public-school students, but represented about 39% of students suspended from school." *Id.*

> "A *New York Times* analysis ...found that Black girls are over five times more likely than white girls to be suspended at least once from school, seven times more likely to receive multiple out-of-school suspensions than white girls and three times more likely to receive referrals to law enforcement."

Erica L. Green, Mark Walker and Eliza Shapiro, " 'A Battle for the Souls of Black Girls'," NYTmes.com, October 1, 2020.

Is this problem all or largely discriminatory disciplinary practices occurring across the country or something else? The *Times* article is based largely on the "victims" explanations of their "victimhood." The referenced evidence of systematic discrimination is weak. If the cause is discrimination, then what do we do? Most schools are government controlled, so political action is possible. But, if much of the cause is with the students, then solutions are significantly more difficult to design and implement.

The biggest factor in crime rates appears to be living in poverty and in disadvantaged neighborhoods.

> "...African Americans and Hispanics... are disproportionately involved in street crime, victimized by street crime, and brought under the control and supervision of the criminal justice system. [But,] **street crimes are more characteristic of impoverished, inner city, and ghetto neighborhoods ... .**"

"Race and Crime—Data Sources And Meaning," *law.JRank.org*, 2020 (emphasis added).

If we had the data, we could look at patterns based upon economic status rather than race. We might find that the patterns of crime statistics are better explained. Of course, Blacks are disproportionately represented among the poor and disadvantaged. But, we must ask: How much of the pattern in school disciplinary actions is the reflection of class or economic, not racial, differences?

So, is any of this evidence of discriminatory racial profiling? Or, does it look like responsible law enforcement, marred by the acts of "bad" or inexperienced cops?

NPR conducted an investigation. "Since 2015, police officers have fatally shot at least 135 unarmed Black men and women nationwide... . NPR reviewed police, court and other records to examine the details of the cases." Cheryl W. Thompson, "Fatal Police Shootings Of Unarmed Black People Reveal Troubling," NPR, January 25, 2021.

The empirical results do not suggest systemic racism:

- "At least 75% of the officers were white. " About what would be expected. ("In hundreds of police departments across the country, the percentage of whites on the force is more than 30 percentage points higher than in the communities they serve... . Minorities make up a quarter of police forces... ." Caroline Cournover, "The Race Gap in America's Police Departments," *Governing*, September 4, 2014.)
- "For at least 15 of the officers, ... the shootings were not their first – or their last... . They have been involved in two – sometimes three or more – shootings."
- "At least six officers had troubled pasts before being hired onto police departments, including drug use and domestic violence. ...Several officers were convicted of crimes while on the force, such as battery, and resisting and obstructing... . More than two dozen officers have racked up citizen complaints or use-of-force incidents."
- "Nineteen of the officers involved in deadly shootings were rookies, with less than a year on the force."

So, individual "bad" or inexperienced cops appear to be much of the problem, participating in 40 of the shootings.

Finally, how is any racial discrimination that exists supposedly embodied in the "system" anyway? Is the fact that police often go where criminal activity is occurring a form of "systemic racism"? Or, is the mere existence of a police force "systemic racism"? That seems to be the view behind the "defunding movement." To me, that position is completely irrational, and I suspect it is not shared by most Black households.

INCOME, HOMEOWNERSHIP AND WEALTH

For many of the comparisons below, we would have wanted to isolate the descendants of Black Americans of the 19th century. Generally, however, we cannot separate out immigrants (or their descendants). The racial categorizations are also self-selected, so the data is not confirmed by objective standards; and, that selection is based largely on choices among the outdated U.S. Census categories. *See, e.g.*, Janet Adamy and Paul Overberg, "The Census Predicament: Counting Americans by Race: The racial and ethnic categories used by the U.S. Census obscure the changing ways we think about identity and assimilation," *WSJ.com*, November 27, 2020. Currently, "[a]mong Black adults, one in eight is an immigrant. ...[And,] Americans of two or more races or ethnicities—including Vice President-elect Kamala Harris—are the country's fastest-growing demographic, and they defy labels." *Id.*

I. *Income*

Median **household** income (in 2017) was as follows:

>Asian $81,331
>White, not Hispanic $68,145
>Hispanic (any race) $50,486
>Black. $40,258

U.S. Census Bureau, *Current Population Survey*, 1968 to 2018 Annual Social and Economic Supplements.

In 2017, the median black **worker**'s income was $31,000. In comparison, for all women, the median was $33,280.

We can look also at the distribution of income within each racial group. For example, comparisons of the thresholds of the top 10% with those of the bottom 10% by income shows significant differences.

> *"In 2016, ... Asians near the top of their income distribution (the 90th percentile) had incomes 10.7 times greater than the incomes of Asians near the bottom of their income distribution (the 10th percentile). The 90/10 ratio among Asians was notably greater than among blacks (9.8), whites (7.8) and Hispanics (7.8)."*

R. Kochhar and A. Cilluffo, "Key findings on the rise in income inequality within America's racial and ethnic groups," *FactTank, Pew Research Center*, July 12, 2018.

> *"[I]f you divide black income into quintiles, the top quintile has now secured almost 50 percent of the total black income, which is a record. The top quintile in the white population has secured about 44 percent of the white income, which is also a record.... if*

> you just look at the distribution of income, **inequality is growing more rapidly in the black community surprisingly than in the white community.** ...[C]mopare the income of black professors and white professors. Black professors make more than white professors. That's because we are in demand. "

William Julius Wilson, PBS, "Interview ... by Henry Louis 'Skip' Gates, Jr.," *Frontline*, November 2015 (emphasis added).

It may be instructive also to look at differences in employment participation rates, reflecting the percentage of persons with or looking for work. That could explain some differences in household income.

> "Among the race and ethnicity groups [for 2016], Native Hawaiians and Other Pacific Islanders (68.7 percent) and **Hispanics (65.8 percent) had the highest labor force participation rates** while American Indians and Alaska Natives (61.1 percent) and **Blacks (61.6 percent) had the lowest participation rates**. The participation rates were 62.9 percent for Whites, 63.2 percent for Asians, and 65.0 percent for people of Two or More Races."

"Labor force characteristics by race and ethnicity, 2016," BLS *Report*, October 2017 (emphasis added).

This income data, based on IRS filings, excludes gains from the underground ("off-the-books") economy and gains from illegal activities such as drug trafficking and prostitution or Ponzi schemes and Medicare fraud. The underground economy is generally estimated at around $2 trillion per year (10-13% of GDP). Drug trafficking is estimated at $100-150 billion per year. ("The results show that drug users in the United States spend on the order of $100 billion annually on all four drugs.... . This figure has been stable over the decade, but there have been important shifts in the drugs being purchased." "How Big Is the U.S. Market for Illegal Drugs?," *rand.org*, 2014.) Prostitution also generates hundreds of billions. of dollars. I have no estimates of the average annual take from all fraudulent activities, but it is very substantial.

If the receipt of that income is not distributed evenly among racial groups, which seems very likely, its inclusion in the calculationwould alter the median and average numbers of the groups differently, perhaps noticeably so. See Sudhir Venkatesh, "The Underground Economy of the Urban Poor," NPR, October 4, 2006. For example, minorities hold a disproportionate number of the jobs in activities readily susceptible to cash payment (and tax evasion), like construction, home maintenance, gardening and housecleaning. The income data also does not include government transfer payments or welfare and public assistance. So, the actual effective (after tax and after government benefits) income differences may be much less than suggested above.

II. *Home ownership*

The current disparity in home ownership is about 30 percentage points, with Black homeownership in the mid-40%s and non-Hispanic white homeownership in the mid-70%s.

Part of the disparity between Black and white non-immigrant Americans appears to derive from national housing policies that started with the Great Depression and continued after World War II. "[F]or decades government policies explicitly helped white Americans build housing capital and denied Black Americans the same opportunity." Gerald F. Seib, "The Debate Over Systemic Racism: Why It Divides and Why It Provides Hope," WSJ.com, July 27, 2020. According to Seib, these programs were not aimed to deprive blacks or minorities, but to maximize the impact of the capital committed by focusing on the "safer" investments:

> "*Starting during the New Deal, the federal government ... began underwriting mortgages to allow working-class Americans to keep their homes during the Depression. But the government wanted to protect its investment by funneling funds to relatively 'safe' mortgages—and decided that homes owned by white people, in all-white neighborhoods, were safer investments than homes sold to Black people or in mixed-race neighborhoods.*"

And, he continues: "[T]he Federal Housing Administration ... simply adopted the same policies. Then, crucially, so did the Veterans Administration when it began helping finance the largest housing boom in American history for soldiers returning from World War II." Id.

The results of these programs, unfortunately, were that Blacks were left behind. Of course, even more white families (by number) were also unable to participate in and benefit from these programs than Blacks.

Such results could have been avoided only by offering subsidies to those left out. In fact, special treatment for housing was then tried:

> "*[T]he Clinton administration decided to expand federal government servicing of low-income and minority borrowers through*

> *various 'affordable-housing goals.' Imposed in 1992, [they] ... requir[ed] a certain percentage of the loans ... acquired each year to have been made to borrowers in financially isolated communities or those who were at or below the median income in the communities in which they lived. ...By 2006, 45 percent of first time homebuyers were putting nothing down."*

Daniel Press,"The Financial Crisis 10 Years Later: Fannie and Freddie Fueled the Subprime Mortgage Bubble," *Competitive Enterprise Institute*, September 12, 2018.

Of course, those efforts largely failed in the end. There is a debate about whether these policies contributed to the housing "bubble"; but, regardless, the bubble burst by 2010. Many of the homeowners who benefitted from the underwriting lower standards lost everything. Ten years later, the Black home ownership percentage is still below where it was in 1968. ("After the foreclosure crisis that accompanied the previous recession, the black homeownership rate slid to 41% in early 2019 from 48% in early 2007." Amara Omeokwe, "Coronavirus Pandemic Threatens to Widen Racial Homeownership Gap," WSJ.com, September 20, 2020.)

So, timing and economic conditions mattered a lot.

A research report by the Urban Institute in 2019 attempted to determine statistically the relationship between various factors and homeownership, controlling for age and some other influences assumed to be independent of race. Jung Hyun Choi, "Breaking Down the Black-White Homeownership Gap," Urban Institute, February 21, 2020. The findings were:

1. "If the household income distribution was the same for white and black households, while other household and MSA level factors remained constant, the gap between the black and white homeownership rates ... would drop by 31 percent, or 9.3 percentage points."
2. "Compared with white households, black households are less likely to marry. If black households were married at the same rate as white households, the black-white homeownership gap ... would decrease by 27 percent, or 8.1 percentage points... ."
3. "Credit score differences: 22 percent of the gap."
4. "Differences in educational attainment do not contribute to the gap."

5. The remaining "unexplained" percentage of the gap was 17% or about 5.7 percentage points.

At least some 49% of the difference in homeownership is attributable to factors not directly related to possible discrimination. Only 31% is attributable to income differences, which might be at least partly the result of discrimination.

In this study, household income appeared to be only slightly more significant than marriage status in explaining the disparities in homeownership. Others have obtained similar results but placed more emphasis on the income gap: "our analysis supports the conclusion that the racial labor income gap is the primary driver behind the large and persistent difference in average wealth between black and white households." Dionissi Aliprantis and Daniel R. Carroll, "What Is Behind the Persistence of the Racial Wealth Gap?" *Federal Reserve Bank of Cleveland*, February 28, 2019.

Of course, as discussed below, there is a strong correlation between household income and marital status.

II. Wealth accumulation

"[T]he 2016 wealth gap [between whites and blacks] is roughly the same as it was in 1962, two years before the passage of the Civil Rights Act of 1964... ." Dionissi Aliprantis and Daniel R. Carroll, "What Is Behind the Persistence of the Racial Wealth Gap?" *Federal Reserve Bank of Cleveland*, February 28, 2019.

Differences in accumulated wealth among racial groups appear to be influenced by several extraneous factors, which should be taken into account in the comparisons. One such factor is the age distribution of the population. Blacks have two thirds the percentage of persons over 54 as whites (23% v. 34%), the age group mostly likely to have accumulated wealth and to pass it to the next generation. (Hispanics have less than half the percentage of whites over 54, 15%.) Carmel Ford."Homeownership by Race and Ethnicity," *Eye On Housing*, December 15, 2017. (However, older Blacks do not have greater wealth than middle aged Blacks.) And, as noted above and discussed below, a much smaller percentage of blacks are married, also adversely affecting wealth accumulation. (About 35% of black women are married, versus 59% of white women and 63% of Asian women. "Marital Status in the United States," Statistical Atlas, September 4, 2018.)

Otherwise, there are some apparent race-related (but not discrimination-related) causes of disparity in accumulated wealth based upon people's behavior on average. Two such factors are are less savings and more conservative investment activity by certain minority groups in comparison to whites:

> "Racial and ethnic differences in housing equity narrow among households in the higher income quartiles, whereas **differences in nonhousing equity generally widen as income increases**. The widening gap in nonhousing equity stems from differences in financial asset holdings, particularly risky assets. At every income quartile and educational level, **the percentage of black and Hispanic households that own risky, higher-yielding assets is considerably smaller** than the percentage of white households."

Sharmila Choudhury, "Racial and Ethnic Differences in Wealth and Asset Choices," *Social Security Bulletin*, Vol. 64, No. 4, 2001/2002 (emphasis added).

Similarly, a study using data from a single very large employer plan found:

> "...both African American and Hispanic employees are less likely to participate in the 401(k) plans. Moreover, ...African Americans contribute a lower proportion of their income to their 401(k) plan on average. ...African Americans and Hispanics tend to draw down on their 401(k) balances more often. Finally, ...both African Americans and Hispanics favor safer assets within their plan options. Together these differences substantially impact the level of 401(k) balances accumulated and therefore overall wealth accumulation."

Kai Yuan Kuan, Mark R. Cullen, and Sepideh Modrek , "Racial Disparities in Savings Behavior for a Continuously Employed Cohort," *NBER Working Paper* No. 20937, February 2015.

Separately, civil disturbances over time have taken a toll on Black wealth, both immediately in destroyed assets and over time in discouragement of investment. "This article examines census data from 1950 to 1980 to measure the riots' impact on the value of central-city residential property, and especially on black-owned property....[E]stimates indicate that the **riots depressed the median value of black-owned property between 1960 and 1970, with little or no rebound in the 1970s**." William J. Collins and Robert A. Margo, "The Economic Aftermath of the 1960s Riots in American Cities: Evidence from Property Values," *The Journal of Economic History*, December 2007, pp. 849-883 (emphasis added).

Nonetheless, as of a few years ago, of the households in the U.S. with a net worth of more than a million dollars, apparently 8% were Black, 8% were Asian and 7% were Hispanic. Some 20% of the millionaires inherited at least some of their wealth. Assuming very few of that 20% were Black, it appears that of those who made it on their own, 10% were Black.

A caveat about immigrants

For many of the matters discussed herein, as noted above, one would like to examine non-immigrant racial categories, because immigrant communities have important different characteristics independent of race.

Many immigrants prioritize helping families at home over savings, explaining differences in savings rates and biasing comparisons of accumulated wealth.

> "A significant share of immigrants all over the world send part of their paycheck back to help their families in their home countries. ...[I]t is estimated that the collective sum of remittance payments in 2017 came to $625 billion, a 7% increase from 2016 .... In the United States alone, it is estimated that more than $148 billion was sent to individuals in other countries in 2017."

Niall McCarthy, "Immigrants In The U.S. Sent Over $148 Billion To Their Home Countries In 2017," *Forbes*, April 8, 2019. "Mexican workers in US are sending record money home despite coronavirus-related economic shutdowns," *The Conversation*, May 27, 2020 ("The 11.2 million people of Mexican origin living in the United States together send upwards of US$38 billion to Mexico each year.")

Also, immigrant communities have lower violent crime rates.

> "Numerous studies show that immigration is strongly associated with lower rates of violent crime. One rigorous study of neighborhoods in Los Angeles in the mid-2000s, for instance, found that greater concentrations of immigrants in a neighborhood are related to significant drops in crime. Similarly, ...analy[sis of] data on Chicago neighborhoods ... found that, after controlling

> *for other factors, concentrated immigration is directly associated with lower rates of violence."*

"Neighborhoods and Violent Crime," *Office of Policy Development and Research*, Summer 2016.

To some extent, the immigrant population is self-selected for success—people who have come affirmatively seeking a better life, risk-takers, people who have fled hardship or oppression and people determined to find opportunities. For example:

> *"...African immigrants are **more likely than Americans overall** to have a college degree, and a recent study ... reveals that their labor-force participation rate is 73%, 10 points higher than that of the overall population. By some measures, Nigerians are the most successful immigrant group in the country. Fifty-nine percent have a college degree, more than double the population as a whole; and in 2018 their median household income was nearly $7,000 higher than the average."*

Dave Seminara, "Africans Knock on America's Door: Why would millions want to immigrate if the U.S. is a land of 'systemic racism'?" *WSJ.com*, September 23, 2020 (emphasis added).

But, immigration status is not an available subcategory of the data from the U.S. Census bureau or other Federal agencies.

So... ?

All of this data may reflect some types of discrimination, just not by race. Indeed, "Black Americans" are not a race. It also indicates that the black racial population consists of at least three distinct groups: immigrants, the middle (and upper) class and the poor (the bottom two quintiles). Our concern should be with this third group: the underprivileged, largely inner-city Blacks.

Harvard sociologist William Julius Wilson explains:

> *"When I said [in 1978] there was **a declining significance of race**, what I really meant was not that racism was declining... but ... that **class was becoming more important than race** in determining individual black life chances. ...[W]e had a tendency to not*

> *pay attention to some of **these non-racial factors that impacted significantly on the black community**.*"

William Julius Wilson. PBS, "Interview ...by Henry Louis 'Skip' Gates, Jr.," November 2015 (emphasis added).

Thus, as we have noted, the Black community is not homogeneous and that the disadvantages noted above exist mainly for the substantial bottom rung.

SOME OTHER FACTS

Here are some facts about the bottom two quintiles of Blacks.

I. MUCH HIGHER RATES OF CRIME AND DRUG USE

> "*...There are many positive things to say about the black community. ... But if you ... don't explain why the murder rate is so high in ... inner city neighborhoods or why the drug addiction rate is so high or why the school dropout rate is so high or **why individual aberrant behavior is so high** in general. If you don't explain those things, you create a void... .*"

William Julius Wilson, PBS, "Interview ... by Henry Louis 'Skip' Gates, Jr.," *Frontline*, November 2015 (emphasis added).

Some of the data on the disparate crime rates is outlined above. The Federal government's War on Crime and War on Drugs led to shockingly high rates of incarceration of Blacks males, but did not reduce crime. So, how do we explain "why individual aberrant behavior is [still] so high" in these disadvantaged Black communities? And, what can be done about it?

II. DE FACTO SEGREGATION

The history and evolution of the current residential segregation is generally as follows:

> "*At the beginning of this century, for Blacks, the typical residential setting was southern and rural; for Whites it was northern and urban....Successive waves of Black migration out of the rural South into the urban North transformed the geographic struc-*

> ture of Black segregation during the twentieth century, however, ending the regional isolation and rural confinement of Blacks."

Douglas S.Massey, "Residential Segregation and Neighborhood Conditions in U.S. Metropolitan Areas," *America Becoming: Racial Trends and Their Consequences: Volume I*, Chapter 13, 2001.

Overall, "... there was a gradual movement of blacks to Northern areas throughout the first half of the twentieth century. And as jobs opened up in Northern industries, there was a fairly rapid increase during the 1940s, so much so that the population of blacks in certain cities quadrupled." William Julius Wilson, PBS, "Interview." Then,

> "[a]fter 1950, Blacks and Whites not only tended to live in different neighborhoods; **increasingly** they lived in different municipalities as well. ...**Blacks and Whites came to reside in wholly different towns and cities.** ...Blacks were still unlikely to come into residential contact with members of other groups. The large ghettos of the North have remained substantially intact ...."

Massey, "Residential Segregation" (emphasis added).

The *de facto* residential separation of races is not easily altered. For example, who moves and to (and from) where? And, how is the relocation of millions of people orchestrated? Presumably, not using the methods of China or of Stalin's Soviet Union. Moreover, mere relocation will not solve the problems.

III. Economically depressed communities

These separate post-1950 Black communities have not been like many Chinatowns across the country–vibrant, active communities attracting tourism and generating economic activity–or, like Harlem, have failed to stay that way. Instead, the *de facto* segregation was accompanied by significant joblessness and high rates of crime, as discussed. These communities have been spiraling downward since the 1950s, turning into islands of despair.

Clearly, joblessness is an important part of the equation. Extensive joblessness infects the whole community. "...a neighborhood in which people are poor and working is entirely different from a neighborhood in which people are poor and jobless. One of the reasons why you have had such an increase in rates of these social dislocations ranging from gang formation to drugs to violent crime is the high jobless rate." William Julius Wilson, PBS, "Interview." Employment has fallen in the inner cities as many companies suffered declines or closed and others moved away. So, "...disadvantaged blacks have really been hard hit by changes in the economy. The computer revolution, changes in scale-based technology. The internationalization of economic activity had combined to decrease the demand for low-skilled workers." Id.

> "...Among adult men (ages 20 and older) ... , Hispanics (76.6 percent) continued to have the highest employment–population ratio. Blacks (62.0 percent) had the lowest, continuing a longstanding pattern. The employment–population ratios for Asian men and White men were 72.8 percent and 69.1 percent, respectively. Among adult women, the ratios showed less variation across the race and ethnicity groups... ."

"Labor force characteristics by race and ethnicity, 2016," BLS *Report*, October 2017.

With respect to unemployment, looking at the 12 months ending October 2020, there are some oddities. For those without a high school diploma, the unemployment for whites and Hispanics were 10.1% and 10.5%, respectively, while the rate for Blacks was 15.3%. In contrast, for persons with a bachelor's degree, the white, Hispanic and Black unemployment rates were 4.8%, 6.7% and 6.1%; and, with advanced degrees, they were 3.3%, 4.2% and 4.4%. So, with more education, Blacks did as well or better than Hispanics. Eric Morath, "Disparity in Jobless Rates Suggests Black Workers Face Slower Recovery," WSJ.com. November 29, 2020.

The isolation of increasingly dysfunctional communities has particularly adverse effects on the children:

> "A rock-bottom housing market, by definition, is always going to exist for people without credit, resources, opportunities or credentials. ...[But,] living in such a place, where everyday survival is often a challenge, is not conducive to acquiring the habits for success in the larger society. .... **About 20% of black children (compared with 1% of white children) grow up in such places.**"

Holman W. Jenkins, Jr., "How to Show That Black Lives Really Matter: The single best thing for young families is leaving a high-crime, high-poverty neighborhood," WSJ.com, July 10, 2020 (emphasis added).

In contrast, "[t]he few areas with small black-white gaps tend to be **low-poverty neighborhoods** with low levels of racial bias among whites and **high rates of father presence** among blacks. Black males who move to such neighborhoods earlier in childhood have significantly better outcomes. However, **less than 5% of black children grow up in such areas**." Raj Chetty, Nathaniel Hendren, Maggie R Jones, Sonya R Porter, "Race and Economic Opportunity in the United States: an Intergenerational Perspective,* The *Quarterly Journal of Economics*, May 2020 (emphasis added).

Again, the Black population is not monolithic. Joblessness and low income are much more prevalent among the urban poor. So, the pertinent questions are how to improve things in the predominantly Black communities, especially for the children, and how to help people who want to escape to do so.

IV. Lack of two-parent households

One of the most serious current challenges for the Black community is the lack of two parent, two wage-earning households, as already noted.

> "More than half (58%) of black children are living with an unmarried parent – 47% with a solo mom. At the same time, 36% of Hispanic children are living with an unmarried parent, as are 24% of white children. The share of Asian children living with unmarried parents is markedly lower (13%)."

Gretchen Livingston, "About one-third of U.S. children are living with an unmarried parent," *Pew Research Center*, April 17, 2018.

> "Women of color are ... much more likely than white women to be raising children while unmarried, even though white women make up the majority of unmarried mothers. In 2016, for example, 40 percent of all births in the United States were to unmarried mothers. This included 17 percent of births to Asian or Pacific Islander women, 29 percent to non-Hispanic white women, 53 percent to Hispanic women, 66 percent to American Indian or Alaskan native women, and 70 percent of births to non-Hispanic black women."

Sarah Jane Glynn, "Breadwinning Mothers Continue To Be the U.S. Norm," *Center for American Progress*, May 10, 2019.

There is pretty wide recognition that children do better in two-parent homes. But, there are economic consequences as well. Marriage boosts home ownership, wealth accumulation and income levels, as well as inheritances. "A recent ... analysis found that 30% of solo mothers and their families are living in poverty compared with 17% of solo father families and 16% of families headed by a cohabiting couple. In comparison, 8% of married couple families are living below the poverty line." Id.

Among Black families, the impact is even starker.

> *"Being raised in a married-couple household led the poverty rate for black children to go down 73 percent compared to mother-only households and 67 percent compared to father-only households. And as evidence of the power of family structure to transcend race, 31 percent of white children raised in mother-only households live in poverty, versus just 12 percent of black children living with their married parents."*

Ian Rowe, "The power of the two-parent home is not a myth," *Thomas B. Fordham Institute*, January 8, 2020.

More generally, the economic benefit of two-parent families is the ability to have dual incomes. In 2012, of all married couples with children under 18, 60% were dual or two-income households, up from 25% in 1960. "The Rise in Dual Income Households," *Pew Research Center*, June 18, 2015. Many affluent families are dual income. See, e.g., Cara David, "Dual income households are the norm in affluent homes," *YouGov.com*, March 08, 2018 ("Fifty-five percent of the affluent households surveyed (those with a household income of at least $150,000) are dual-income households"). For example, these various studies show that Asians have the greatest percentage of married, two-parent households, the highest household income and the lowest crime rates, well ahead of non-Hispanic whites in all categories.

This problem is not new; it was identified over 50 years ago.

> *"the Moynihan Report [1965] highlighted the fact that the Negro family was weakening as reflected in the growth of female-headed households, and that the growth of female-headed households would have profound negative implications for the black family, because female-headed families are much more vulnerable to problems in the larger society, much more likely to be*

> *impoverished, and much more likely to experience difficulty in socializing children to compete in the broader society. ...Single-parent families, family break-ups in the black community are problematic because of the impact on children, and that's the main thing. ... So, children growing up in these poor, female-headed families are at a disadvantage ... ."*

Ben Wattenberg, *The First Measured Century* on PBS: *The Other Way of Looking at American History,* "William Julius Wilson Interview," 2000.

At the same time, the lack of two parent households is not a legacy of slavery or even of Jim Crow. The percentage of two-parent households among Blacks, as reflected in the U.S. Census, exceeded that for whites consistently between 1890 and 1940. Walter E. Williams, *Race and Economics: How Much Can Be Blamed on Discrimination?* (2011), p.8 (citing Thomas Sowell's research).

William Julius Wilson points to joblessness as a cause of single parent households.

> *"[W]e found ... a strong relationship between black male joblessness and single-parent families. ...[T]hat employed fathers were two-and-a-half times more likely to marry the mother of their first child than jobless fathers. This is especially true of men under the age of thirty-five. So, in the inner city we found a very strong relationship between male joblessness and female-headed families. ...Moynihan [in1965] talked about [how]... joblessness creates problem streams in the family. It leads to family break-ups resulting in an increasing number of families going on welfare."*

Wattenberg, "Interview."

However, the lack of two-parent households will not be cured merely by providing jobs for the currently unemployed, many of whom are effectively unemployable. The focus must be on the young--on children and young adults. There must be hope and opportunity for the young, looking to the future.

So, is this factor a problem that can or should be addressed or is it just a partial explanation for the observed disparities?

V. Deteriorating public education

"[T]he black lives most at risk are the young men and women living in the nation's poorest urban neighborhoods, attending the worst-performing public schools in the U.S." Daniel Henninger, "Reading the Trump-Biden Inkblots: Voters can't pretend a Biden presidency will help the black children trapped in failing inner-city schools," *WSJ.com*, July 29, 2020 (emphasis added)

The consequences are clear and dramatic.

'Blacks make up just over 1% of all SAT test takers who score between 700 and 800 on the math SAT, but 24% of all math SAT test takers with scores between 300 and 390. The average black math SAT score (454 in 2020) is more than a standard deviation below the average Asian math SAT score and nearly a standard deviation below the average white math score." Heather MacDonald, "Woke Science Is an Experiment Certain to Fail: Advancing knowledge, not imposing diversity, should be the goal of federal research funding.," *WSJ.com*, September 24, 2020.

Yet, today's response is: "many people would say that the fact that, on average, black students do not perform as highly on standardized tests as white students means that the tests are racist, in that they disadvantage black students." John McWhorter, "The Dictionary Definition of Racism Has to Change," *The Atlantic*, June 22, 2020. However, presumably no one suggests that the SATs were designed or have been utilized to discriminate against Blacks. Is the solution to this disparity to abolish the use of SATs? Really? That is a solution to what?

Can, perhaps, instead, something be done about the schools? At least, politicians could resist the union pressures against educational alternatives and experimentation and the belief that more money is an answer to what is wrong. Perhaps, they could even make changes that would actually help.

Again, citing work by Thomas Sowell, Walter Williams observed that the disgraceful state of Black schools is a relatively recent phenomenon:

> "[Baltimore's] *Frederick Douglass High School of yesteryear produced many distinguished alumni, such as Thurgood Marshall and Cab Calloway, and several judges, congressmen, and civil*

> rights leaders....[It] was second in the nation in black Ph.D.s among its alumni. As early as 1899, [Paul Laurence Dunbar High School, a black public school in Washington, D.C.] ... students scored higher on citywide tests than any of the city's white schools. From its founding in 1870 to 1955, most of its graduates went off to college. ...[Its] distinguished alumni include U.S. Sen. Edward Brooke, physician Charles Drew, and, during World War II, nearly a score of majors, nine colonels and lieutenant colonels, and a brigadier general. Today's Paul Laurence Dunbar and Frederick Douglass high schools have material resources that would have been unimaginable to their predecessors. However, having those resources have meant absolutely nothing in terms of academic achievement."

"The Tragedy of Black Education Is New," *TheDailySignal*, December 2, 2020.

There are indications of potential routes to progress.

> "...[C]harter schools are not simply doing a better job than their :traditional counterparts with the same demographic groups. In many cases, inner-city charter-school students are outperforming their peers in the wealthiest and whitest suburban school districts in the country. ...[Moreover, quoting economist Thomas Sowell,] '[t]he educational success of these charter schools undermines theories of genetic determinism, claims of cultural bias in the tests, assertions that racial "integration" is necessary for blacks to reach educational parity and presumptions that income differences are among the "root causes" of educational differences'."

Jason L. Riley, "Thomas Sowell Has Been Right From the Start: His latest book on charter schools continues his research on minority success in education," *WSJ.com*, July 21, 2020.

The existence of some choice and the feeling of influence with respect tp one's children's education are highly desirable and are likely to lead to better results. But, public policy has been counterproductive, discouraging charter schools and discriminating against parochial schools, apparently in the interest of equality. Similarly, during this pandemic, alternative approaches to continuing education are resisted in the interests of "equality", because they may disadvantage the poorer students. Vested interests are being protected at the expense of the children. See, e.g., Elliot Kaufman, "The Teachers Union's Tiny New Enemy: The behemoth National

Education Association seeks to squash popular pandemic microschools," WSL.com, October 14, 2020 ("It's a strange pitch from the teachers union: Microschools are dangerous—they help their students learn more! This seems like a reason to broaden access, not restrict it"). At the same time, although everyone seems to recognize that lack of in-person instruction hurts the underprivileged students more, those same vested interests resist resumption of in-class instruction even well into 2021.

When the accepted approach has resulted in decades of failure, that is not a reason for "more of the same" in bigger doses; it is a reason for change—a reason for experimentation, innovation and diversity. However, we will now experience a reassertion of the influence of the teachers' union under President-elect Biden. Let us hope that we see some improvements and gains, that more money actually does something positive.

GOVERNMENT POLICIES

The review above of various relevant factors suggests that the real problems plaguing the disadvantaged segment of Black Americans today are a lack of mobility (physical and economic), a predominance of single-parent families and largely dysfunctional communities, with high rates of crime and violence (by Blacks against Blacks). Racism simply is not the biggest problem for these Blacks nor the primary cause of their current levels of poverty.

Moreover, as noted, these problems arose long after slavery ended and even after Jim Crow. Indeed, they followed the reduction in legalized racism and the *de jure* integration after World War II. We need to identify the causes of these changes after 1950. The current narratives about "systemic racism" offer no insights into this question. We also need to know why these problems —as also previously noted, already identified and described in the late 1960s—have persisted and become more severe.

So, what has government done with respect to the well-being of these communities over the past 60 years and with what effect?

I. SOCIAL WELFARE

Over the past 55 years, since the beginning of The Great Society programs in 1964, we have spent over $20 trillion (in today's dollars) on fighting poverty. Yet, we still have poverty.

Why?

Because the money was provided for current consumption, not infrastructure, and it was then spent, not saved. As a result, these programs merely ameliorated the burdens of poverty, which has tended to make poverty more resilient. They reduced "poverty" (as then defined), but did not help the recipients to escape dependence on government subsidies, to become more self-sufficient and independent.

Policy makers failed to realize the extent to which making poverty more tolerable would reduce the incentives to escape poverty and would tend to increase dependency on the state.

> *"The ... programs are focused on making poverty more comfortable – giving poor people more food, better shelter, health care, etc. – rather than giving people the tools that will help them escape poverty. As a result, we have been successful in reducing the worst privations of poverty. Few Americans live with out the basic necessities of life, yet neither do they rise out of poverty. Moreover, their children are also likely to be poor."*

Michael D. Tanner, "War on Poverty at 50 – Despite Trillions Spent, Poverty Won," CATO *Institute*, January 8, 2014.

As Tanner observes: "Our goal should not be a society where people struggle along in poverty, dependent on government for just enough to survive, but rather a society where as few people as possible live in poverty, and where every American can reach his or her full potential."

Similarly, Jason Riley argues that:

> *"[g]overnment programs are no substitute for the development of human capital. If wealth-redistribution schemes lifted people out of poverty, we would have closed these gaps a long time ago. Liberal politicians and activists have little interest in addressing the ways in which black behavioral choices impact inequality."*

"The Race Card Has Gone Bust: America has never been fairer or more integrated, yet politicians obsess over wiping out discrimination," WSJ.com, July 16, 2019.

The basic social problems of disintegrating families and communities were identified by social scientists beginning in the 1960s, but minimal ameliorative actions were taken by government to address them.

> "In 1965 Daniel Patrick Moynihan, then an assistant secretary of labor, issued a detailed report concluding that generational poverty among black Americans was the result not of an insufficiently generous welfare system but of the black family's dissolution. He was dismissed as a racist. Irving Kristol, James Q. Wilson and others argued for decades that an unreformed welfare state hurt minority communities more than they helped...."

Barton Swaim, "Radicals Have a Point About Racial Liberalism: They know the prevailing orthodoxy has failed. Too bad they don't recall those who predicted its failure," WSJ.com, August 9, 2020.

In fact, the incentive structures created by government policies aggravate and perpetuate the disparities. It is as if these isolated Black communities have been written off and bought off with increasing handouts.

II. Racial preferences

Similarly, affirmative action is largely irrelevant to Black inner-city youth. Racial preferences have aided the Black middle class in competition with the white middle class, but have done little for the really disadvantaged. The same is true of the recent proposals to forgive student debt and of the current efforts to increase diversity on corporate boards and among CEOs. Or, the actions to increase substantially the minimum wage; whether or not such actions will increase unemployment, they clearly will not generate jobs for the currently unemployed.

Of course, affirmative action programs may have improved the educational experiences for others (of all races) by increasing diversity and broadening outlooks and these current efforts may enhance and enrich our institutions and society. (Harvard's express justification for its admission policy may be sound policy, whether it actually reflects the motivation.)

But, have they helped or hurt Black Americans as a group on balance?

Good queston.

One answer:

> "[In the 1960s and 1970s,] ... policy makers ... blessed the creation of racial and ethnic categories and the related use of racial preferences for university admissions, employment and government

> *contracting. The formalizing of groups, the addition of incentives to adhere to them, and the culture of victimhood that the whole scheme instilled, betrayed the colorblind promise of the civil-rights movement ...[and]* **all but ensured victimhood would never end.**"

Mike Gonzalez, "We Might Get Fooled Again: The policy mistakes of the 1960s and '70s laid the foundation for the identity politics of today," WSJ.com, July 9, 2020 (emphasis added).

III. AND NOW?

So, have we learned anything?

It appears not. The new current (2021) approach is substantially to expand government social benefits, divorcing them from work and, even, from need. Minorities are helped only incidentally. The programs are squarely aimed at the middle class.

The so-called "Covid-19 Relief" bill allocated less than 30% of its spending for assistance to persons who actually suffered economically from the pandemic. Benefits went to government employees, pubic school teachers and staff of professional service organizations who generally continued to be paid while working fewer hours, often from home, saving the time and expense of commuting, and enjoying greater flexibility and personal time. And, President Biden now rewards them with a substantial pay increase. For those with government student loans, payments were suspended. Economically, all of these people are better off as a result of the pandemic; yet, they got the government "relief" funds. And, more than $100 billion went to state governments that are enjoying record surpluses. Relief? And, how much simply went to fraudsters and crooks?

Of course, millions were put out of work by the pandemic, especially in the hospitality and travel industries. But, the government provided substantially increased unemployment payments, giving many an income from not working that was greater than their income while employed and inviting massive numbers of fraudulent filings pursuant to which some 10-15% of the benefits nationwide were stolen, and even more in California. The bill even provided a tax exemption for over $10,000 of unemployment benefits per person. However, a household would have to earn about $75,000 for the year to benefit from that exemption (i.e., one would have to be in the top third of all families).

Who are to be the primary beneficiaries of this bill? Not the poor.

The two quarters with the highest GDP growth in the last 40 years are 3Q 2020 and 1Q 2021. Household net worth grew 16% in the 15 months ending March 31, 2021. Even the net worth of the bottom quintile grew 2.5%. Individual savings rates have soared, credit card debt has plummeted and there are record unfilled job openings—all evidencing that much of the benefits went to persons not seriously in need. As a further irony, the bill appears to have fueled rapid, dramatic inflation, which will hurt savers, those on fixed incomes and most average workers. Not so much those living on government benefits or the wealthy. Just the average working people.

The response? Plans to spend another $3.5-5.5 trillion! The President assures us that the inflation is just "transitory" (so is life) and that his program will pay for itself and cost "nothing". These are deceptions of Trumpian proportions. The Build Back Better proposal is rife with budgetary gimmicks, not for overcoming procedural technicalities, as is usual; but, to deceive the American public.

The President's so-called "infrastructure" bill would have devoted less than 30% of its commitments to capital investment or infrastructure. The rest was for current consumption. And, the proposed "American Rescue" and the "American Families" plans do not even purport to focus on Blacks or on minorities or, even, on the bottom quintile, but are intended to extend government subsidy payments to more than 50% of all voters. The proposal is to do so initially at the expense of the top 1%. Of course, with this "shotgun" approach, some of the benefits will go to the needy, but at huge cost.

These plans are simply efforts to "buy" votes. The political motivation must be the belief that few Americans will have the strength to vote against continued handouts to themselves at the expense of others. Will it work? We shall see. But, I am pretty sure it would not have worked if announced in advance. If Biden had disclosed during the campaign what he would do when elected (assuming he had any idea), he would have lost the election. But, I believe he did not back then have a clue what he would be doing now if elected (and may still not).

And, So... ?

Racists and racism continue to exist and have a negative and disruptive impact on American society, but the national identity simply is no longer racist. Look at Blacks in government (mayors, police chiefs, governors, senators and, even, President and Vice-President), business, entertainment and sports or their presence at universities, in the military and among the ranks of millionaires (some hundreds of thousands) and even of billionaires (12 or 13 worldwide, at least 7 in the United States)—there are more Black millionaires in America than in the rest of the world combined.

Here are the comments by four Black American authors and educators:

- Ward Connerly. "The claim that America is 'systemically racist' is a false narrative that fuels racial paranoia, division and hatred. If we can identify specific institutions or people within them that are racist, we should confront them. If not, it doesn't serve us well to allow a false presumption of guilt to guide our conduct." "America Isn't a Racist Country," WSJ.com, July 24, 2020.
- Robert L. Woodson Sr. "Those who attribute all failure of blacks in America—academic, occupational and even moral—to an all-purpose invisible villain of 'institutional racism' are betraying those they purport to represent. ... This debilitating dynamic is exacerbated by the guilt among white liberals, who approach the black community with a combination of pity, patronage and pandering." "The Resilience of the Black American," WSJ.com, August 6, 2020.
- Shelby Steele. "... we blacks aren't much victimized any more. Today we are free to build a life that won't be stunted by racial persecution. Today we are far more likely to encounter racial preferences than racial discrimination. Moreover, we live in a society that generally shows us goodwill—a society that has isolated racism as its most unforgivable sin." "The Inauthenticity Behind Black Lives Matter," WSJ.com, November 22, 2020.
- And, economist Walter Williams, in his 2011 book *Race and Economics: How Much Can Be Blamed on Discrimination?*, argued that the difficulties of poor Blacks are not due to racial discrimination but are "self-inflicted ... or a result of policies, programs, and regulations emanating from federal, sate and local governments" (p.10).

I suggest that the continuing problems are not the result of current racism nor, even, of historical racism. They are significantly the result of the well-intentioned but misguided or naive governmental social policies that permitted and even encouraged the expansion of bad behavior. Such programs include social welfare in a wide variety of forms, public housing and racial preferences. These policies have created a culture and preserved a societal structure that disadvantage minorities, especially Blacks. These policies have eroded the values of family and community.

The current obsession with systemic racism is not helpful. It is a false narrative that deflects attention from the real struggles, further discourages ambition and self-reliance and indulges those who want to feel guilty. The principe problems affecting inner-city Blacks, identified above, were not caused by systemic racism, and they will not be solved by the diminution or even elimination of systemic racism.

There are two ways to reduce inequality: pull up the disadvantaged or pull down the successful. The latter is certainly easier to accomplish; and, unfortunately, there is considerable political support for that approach, especially in education. "If it is not available to all, it should not be available to any." Really? Progress is almost always incremental, in steps, "Trickle up" (and "trickle down") is evident and effective in many spheres of life. We will always have a bottom 10% and a bottom quintile. (And, a top 1%.) The important issue is how fluid and dynamic those groups are. Inequality causes ambition in some have-nots and envy in others. It is no surprise which ones tend to succeed and which ones tend to fail. There need to be opportunities to succeed, and to fail. We want equal opportunity; but, inequality In outcome is not necessarily inequitable nor equal outcomes, equitable.

From the politicians' standpoint, a hand-out is much easier to offer than a hand-up. Sadly, it is also often easier to accept, and it can become addictive. One thinks of the movement to de-criminalize drugs—the likely result would be fewer criminals but not fewer addicts. This approach is a perversion of paternalism—it is not "paternal", but patronizing—and it is patronization at its worst. Patronization and indulgence soothe the consciences of the privileged. They also are approaches that are politically easier to design, adopt and support. But, such approaches exacerbate and perpetuate, not ameliorate, the problems.

But, what is also needed is that which we often call "tough love," consisting of ample support coupled with high expectations and a clear emphasis on personal responsibility—opportunities combined with consequences, opportunities to succeed and to fail. So, government, especially Federal government, is not well-suited to address these problems. It has great difficulties (practical and legal) with accountability and differentiation. The better approach is through private actions, by both charitable and for-profit entities. Government may provide support and incentives. Correction of the problems will probably have to be incremental, person by person and family by family. We cannot simply improve permanently everyone's lot across the board by sweeping governmental action.

Some promising government avenues for improvement are: (i) subsidies for the employment of persistently unemployed persons in the inner-cities, (ii) policies that provide incentives to individual savings and productive investment by underprivileged families, (iii) targeted programs to assist young families in escaping the inner-city neighborhoods and (iv) increased choice and flexibility in grade school and high school education. These are matters for state and local governments–not for the Federal government. And, such steps would be surprisingly inexpensive.

But, the real need is for the creation of healthy neighborhoods communities. For example, it appears that "on April 1, 2010, 44 percent of the low-income black men from the Watts neighborhood of central Los Angeles were incarcerated. On the other hand, just 6.2 percent of the men who grew up with similar incomes in the Compton neighborhood were incarcerated on that day. Compton is just 2.3 miles from Watts." David Brooks, *The Second Mountain* (2019),p.273. That is something only local governments and local groups can do.

Advice to my Children

Dear Children:

Over the past month, I've seen at least two articles suggesting that parents should try to write down things they would like to say to their children when they (the parents) are gone.

I must say that, in the contemplation of such an exercise, the recommendation seems almost incomprehensible. I am not sure that there is anything I would want to say to you two after I am gone. What I would want is to be able to be there for you in bad times and (inconspicuously, obviously) during good times. There is nothing to be said or done to achieve that wish.

So, instead, I have been thinking about what I would like to say to you now. I think that it is time to try to say what I want to say. But, I recognize that were I to try to do so orally, I would be constantly interrupted with comments and arguments; and, with my strength and voice both declining, it will be easier for me to do so this way.

Here goes.

First,

I hope that each of you make space in your lives for the spiritual. I have come to realize that I strongly believe that there is something "more" than what we normally see and perceive. I am not sure that it offers any comfort or promises or, even, anything particularly relevant to our lives on Earth or to our "souls". It may be that that which is beyond our current grasp and understanding may truly be and remain forever incomprehensible. But, the fact (if I may call it that) that there is something beyond our world, something transcendent, seems to me to open an important additional dimension to our experiences of this life.

I am quite sure that this "more" bears little resemblance to any of the established religions. Nonetheless, I am in favor of established religions because I believe that the opportunity to worship, aspire and feel as part of a community is useful and desirable. Clearly, some of the spiritual experience can and must be achieved alone and in solitude. But, to me there is an important part of it that exists in the gathering of people seeking to be better people and professing that goal: the feelings of community, of shared compassion and of professed aspirations. Whether alone or in a group, I hope that you can open yourself to gain some glimpse of that "more".

Second,

I hope that each of you has the experience of committing yourself utterly, totally, all-consumingly to some project or undertaking. The reason is so that you can experience the achievement of something beyond what you think you can do and, even after the fact, what you can believe that you did do. For some period, forget the comfortable, the convenient and the easy. Then, throw yourself into something.

This probably seems a bit convoluted, but I'm referring to some experiences that I had in my own life—experiences that affected me profoundly. They occurred a few times during my work and then again in the writing of the book. They were times in which my concentration and focus utterly blocked out the rest of the world and the other things that constantly go on in one's mind. The result, in each case, was that I was able to do things beyond what appeared to be the limits of my abilities, to transcend the plane in which I normally operate, to perform like someone else or some other being.

I know it sounds weird, but there were two signs after the fact that something unusual had happened. First, I would have a feeling of disorientation and almost a lack of memory. Second, when I looked at what I had, in these cases, written, I found not only that I could not believe that I had done it, but, sometimes, I wasn't sure I even understood it.

"Transcend" is really the important notion. It is the idea that through total concentration and focus, one is able to reach beyond the normal, everyday experiences and attain something supra-normal. By the way, this idea may but does not necessarily tie to my comments about spirituality. For example, I know that it is possible that the human brain has capacities vastly beyond those of which we make use. There may be other levels of existence that are attainable purely on a materialistic basis.

As hiring partner, I was regularly asked by applicants whether I had enough time to do everything I wanted. Obviously, the answer was "no"! If one did, then one clearly did not want enough. If you are not making sacrifices and trade offs, then you are short changing yourself. Challenges bring more achievement and rewards.

Third,

Be prudent: keep a "safety net". But also, seek adventure and excitement. You can "afford" to take some risks. It would be foolish not to do so.

My goal has been to assure that both of you will be free from the burdens and constraints arising from financial considerations. Not to provide leisure and luxury, but to give freedom and opportunity. I want you not to know the anxiety and worry that can arise from challenges to make "ends meet". Such worries, like the fear that some unexpected emergency will create a financial crisis, seem to me to be highly destructive of the human spirit, even though such worries are the lot of most of mankind. Similarly, I hope to leave both of you in the position where you will not feel "forced" to accept professional or personal circumstances that destroy your spirit because of financial factors.

As one of you already knows, I very much want you both are able to avoid the quagmire in which I found myself. Of course, I was not confronting financial hardship as the cost of freeing myself, only less of what I had and of what I thought I wanted. So, I guess one would say it was covetousness and envy over material possessions that, at least in part, kept me from taking care of myself and my children. I do not feel good about that. It has been a source of regret, but I have been trying to live differently in recent years.

If there were a way to teach you not to care too much about material things, that would be the greater gift. But, in the absence of an ability to do that, I have sought what seems to me to be the next best thing–giving you security and the ability to have as much indulgence as one could reasonably want. You will be able to lead full lives of opportunity without financial insecurity.

I know that the money does not guarantee satisfied or happy lives, but it is usually better to have it.

Finally,

I would like to tell you to include playfulness in your lives, to make room for some silliness. It provides some sparkle and encourages humility and perspective. But, what is the point? One of you already does, and the other probably never will.

I guess that's life.

Take care of yourself and of each other. Please.

I love you,

Dad

www.ingramcontent.com/pod-product-compliance
Lightning Source LLC
Chambersburg PA
CBHW052047070526
44584CB00017B/2092